Green Church

Caretakers
of
God's Creation

Daphna Flegal

Suzann Wade

Abingdon Press

Nashville

Green Church
Caretakers of God's Creation

Daphna Flegal lives in Nashville where she is a writer and editor of children's
curriculum resources. She is a diaconal minister in West Michigan Conference
of The United Methodist Church, where she served in local congregations as
Director of Children's Ministries and Director of Christian Eductation. She
presently serves as lead editor for children's resources at The United Methodist
Publishing House. She is joyously awaiting the birth of her very first grandchild.

Suzann Wade lives in beautiful Oklahoma City with her husband, Daniel, and two
amazing kids, Madeline and Sean. Having spent more than a decade in children's
ministry, she still searches each day for new ways to help God's children of all ages
experience God's presence all around them every day. As a self proclaimed non-
outdoorsy type with a brown thumb, Suzann also longs to help others like herself,
less talented in the outdoor ways, to embrace, celebrate and care for the wonderful
and even creepy parts of God's glorious creation. Suzann also believes we should
always remember every child we meet was created with the image/imagination of
God, and each one has so much to teach us about God and caring for God's creation
if we will only ask them and then give them a chance to dream, explore, and share.

PACP00579979-01

ISBN 978-1-426-70770-4

10 11 12 13 14 15 16 17 18 19—10 9 8 7 6 5 4 3 2 1

Printed in the U. S. A.

FSC
Mixed Sources
Product group from well-managed
forests, controlled sources and
recycled wood or fiber
Cert no. SCS-COC-002484
www.fsc.org
©1996 Forest Stewardship Council

CONTENTS

Your church can do a church-wide study of Green Church by using the youth resource, *Burst: Green Church*, and the adult resource, *Green Church: Reduce, Reuse, Recycle, Rejoice!* by Rebekah Simon-Peter, along with *Green Church: Caretakers of God's Creation* for children.

Recycle Songs

And God Saw that It Was Good
Tune: The Farmer in the Dell

God saw that it was good. (clap, clap)
God saw that it was good. (clap, clap)
God made the sun and moon and stars,
And saw that it was good. (clap, clap)

God saw that it was good. (clap, clap)
God saw that it was good. (clap, clap)
God made the sky and sea and earth,
And saw that it was good. (clap, clap)

God saw that it was good. (clap, clap)
God saw that it was good. (clap, clap)
God made the seeds and plants and trees,
And saw that it was good. (clap, clap)

God saw that it was good. (clap, clap)
God saw that it was good. (clap, clap)
God made the fish and birds and cows,
And saw that it was good. (clap, clap)

God saw that it was good. (clap, clap)
God saw that it was good. (clap, clap)
God made me and God made you,
And saw that it was good. (clap, clap)

God saw that it was good. (clap, clap)
God saw that it was good. (clap, clap)
God rested on the seventh day,
And saw that it was good. (clap, clap)

Based on Genesis 1
Words: Daphna Flegal
Words © 2000 Cokesbury

Jump, Turn, Praise
Tune: Pick a Bale of Cotton

Gonna jump down, turn around,
(Jump; turn around.)
Clap my hands and praise God.
(Clap hands; raise arms.)
Jump down, turn around,
(Jump; turn around.)
Clap my hands and praise!
(Clap hands; raise arms.)

Gonna jump down, turn around,
(Jump; turn around.)
Stomp my feet and praise God.
(Stomp feet; raise arms.)
Jump down, turn around,
(Jump; turn around.)
Stomp my feet and praise!
(Stomp feet; raise arms.)

Gonna jump down, turn around,
(Jump; turn around.)
Pat my head and praise God.
(Pat head; raise arms.)
Jump down, turn around,
(Jump; turn around.)
Pat my head and praise!
(Pat head; raise arms.)

Gonna jump down, turn around,
(Jump; turn around.)
Swing my hips and praise God.
(Swing hips; raise arms.)
Jump down, turn around,
(Jump; turn around.)
Swing my hips and praise!
(Swing hips; raise arms.)

Gonna jump down, turn around,
(Jump; turn around.)
Shake myself and praise God.
(Wiggle whole body; raise arms.)
Jump down, turn around,
(Jump; turn around.)
Shake myself and praise!
(Wiggle whole body; raise arms.)

Words: Daphna Flegal
Words © 2001 Abingdon Press

Psalm 8:6
Tune: God Is so Good

You let us rule. You let us rule.
You let us rule what your hands have made.

Words: Psalm 8:6, adapted

Down in the Dump

Tune: Down by the Bay

Down in the dump,
Where the garbage grows and grows,
Back to my home
I dare not go
For if I do,
My mother will say,
"Did you see a plastic bag, waving like a flag?
Down in the dump."

Down in the dump,
Where the garbage grows and grows,
Back to my home
I dare not go
For if I do,
My mother will say,
"Did you see an old tin can, playing in the band?
Did you see a plastic bag, waving like a flag?
Down in the dump."

Down in the dump,
Where the garbage grows and grows,
Back to my home
I dare not go
For if I do,
My mother will say,
"Did you see a styrofoam cup, running from a pup?
Did you see an old tin can, playing in the band?
Did you see a plastic bag, waving like a flag?
Down in the dump."

Continue adding rhymes:
"Did you see a rubber tire, singing in the choir?"
"Did you see a worn out shoe, walking to the zoo?"
"Did you see a cardboard box, talking to an ox?"
"Did you see a box of soap, jumping with a rope?"
"Did you see a jelly jar, driving in a car?"

Words: Daphna Flegal

The Trash That Gets Into the Ocean

Tune: My Bonnie Lies Over the Ocean

The trash that gets into the ocean
Is killing the fish, can't you see?
So please put a stop to pollution,
And clean up the rivers and seas.

Clean up! Clean up!
O clean up the rivers and seas, oh please!
Clean up! Clean up!
O clean up the rivers and seas.

Words: Daphna Flegal

Recycle What You Can

Tune: The Farmer in the Dell

Recycle what you can,
Recycle what you can,
Paper, plastics, glass, and tin,
Recycle what you can.

Words: Daphna Flegal

The More That We Save Water

Tune: The More We Get Together

The more that we save water,
save water, save water,
The more that we save water, the happier we'll be.
So turn off the water when you brush your teeth clean.
The more that we save water, the happier we'll be.

The more that we save water,
save water, save water,
The more that we save water, the happier we'll be.
So step in the shower instead of the bathtub.
The more that we save water, the happier we'll be.

Words: Daphna Flegal

If You're Green and You Know It

Tune: If You're Happy and You Know It

If you're green and you know it, plant a tree.
If you're green and you know it, plant a tree.
If you're green and you know it,
then your life will surely show it.
If you're green and you know it, plant a tree.

If you're green and you know it…
turn off lights.
save a whale.
sort the trash.
ride a bike.
love the earth.

Words: Daphna Flegal

In the Beginning
Be Green • think Green

Objectives

The children will
• hear the biblical story of Creation;
• recognize that God wants us to be good stewards of creation;
• learn that being a good steward means to take personal responsibility for taking care of the earth;
• experience ways to take care of creation.

Bible Story

Genesis 1:1-28, 31a: the story of Creation, including human beings' responsibility for taking care of what God has created.

Bible Verse

Psalm 8:6, CEV: You let us rule over everything your hands have made.

Focus for the Teacher

God Is the Creator of All

Many of us have heard the Creation story many times. Because we know it so well, we are at risk of overlooking one of the most profound statements of faith in the entire Bible: "In the beginning, God created" (Genesis 1:1a).

The Bible begins with God and the simple, but astonishing, fact that God is the Creator.

Genesis 1 teaches the following:
• God is the Creator of all;
• All life comes from God and depends on God;
• People are in charge of creation;
• God sees creation as very good;
• God rested.

All comes from God. God created the far reaches of the universe and the ground just outside your door. God created the largest stars and the smallest amoeba. In creation, we glimpse the magnitude of God.

All Life Comes From God

Life is a gift, a part of God's plan in creation. From the beginning of time, life originates from God and depends on God. God is the source and sustainer of everything.

People Are in Charge of Creation

In Genesis 1:26 and 1:28, God gives people "dominion" over creation. The Hebrew word *radah* used here means to rule. The word is used in other Scriptures to refer to the rule of a king or of God. Rulers can be self-serving or rulers can be benevolent. Which type of ruler applies here? Some say this verse gives people permission to use creation any way they choose. However, most scholars say that the dominion being given here is intended to reflect God's rule over us. God is not self-serving. God is generous and cares for us. So we are to be generous to creation and care for it.

The command given to humans in the second telling of the Creation story echoes this. "The LORD God took the man and put him in the garden of Eden to till it and keep it" (Genesis 2:15). The word used as keep in this verse is the Hebrew word, *shamar*. Shamar means to keep, guard, or provide for. God tells Noah to shamar, or keep the animals on his ark (Genesis 6:19).

From the beginning, God asked humans to care for one another and for all creation. Some have said the purpose of humanity was to act as caretakers or stewards of creation. The basis of all stewardship can be traced back to our creation.

God Sees Creation as Very Good

At the end of each stage of Creation, God says it is good. After charging humans with the care of creation, God looks at all creation and says it is VERY good. God is pleased with creation and the way it is designed to work.

Creation is interdependent. Humans depend on creation for nourishment, and creation depends on us to keep and protect God's created order.

God Rested

God's rest serves as the basis for two central elements of faith. First, rest is a necessary and sacred part of life. God's day of rest established the practice of the sabbath, a weekly sacred day of rest. As Christians, we remember the sabbath and teach our children how this rest helps us serve and honor God.

Second, many scholars say God's day of rest demonstrates the faith God has in creation. God is an ever-present part of creation, but God chooses not to keep tinkering with it. God has faith creation will work. (Even in the story of the flood, found later in Genesis, God shows faith in creation by saving Noah's family and the animals.)

The tendency, when discussing our need to care for the earth, is to focus on negative facts. When people focus on negative statistics, reality seems grim. People feel frustrated and overwhelmed.

However, when we focus on Genesis 1, we see a very different reality. We discover our potential, and we find hope. The world is full of new ideas and solutions. We show our children that God and the church both have faith in their abilities to improve the world through acts of stewardship, and we help them claim their call to be caretakers of creation.

the Bible in these Lessons

Psalm 8:6, CEV
The Bible verse for these six weeks is from Psalm 8: "You let us rule everything your hands have made."

You let us rule everything your hands have made.

Psalm 8:6, CEV

The New Revised Standard Version translates "rule over" as "dominion." Either translation will need to be explained. Neither "rule over" nor "dominion" means being given unlimited control and a freedom to use God's creation in ways that serve selfish needs rather than serving the needs of the created world and the needs of people. These words include a sense of responsibility and care.

Another word we want to teach the children is the word *steward*. A steward takes personal responsibility for something in his or her care. One synonym for steward is keeper. A steward of God's creation is a keeper of the earth.

Genesis 1:1-28, 31a
According to Genesis 1 God made creation in seven stages. On the first day God created light and dark. On the second day God created the sky and the waters. On the third day God created the moon, the sun, and the stars. On the fourth day God created the land and the seas, as well as vegetation. On the fifth day God created the living creatures in the oceans and in the air. On the sixth day God created all the living creatures on the land including humans.

After God created all else, God created humans. God made man and woman in the image of God. God breathed into humans and gave them life. God showed humans the majesty of creation and gave them the responsibility of caring for it. Then God called creation very good. On the final day of the Creation story, God rested.

About the Children

Children are concrete thinkers. They may wonder why you are painting the church green. Help them understand that you are not talking about the color *green*. Instead the word *green* is used to help us remember a special way we can take care of the earth. When we feed wild birds, pick up trash, recycle, or plant a tree, we are being green. Being green is one way we show love for God and say thank you for God's awesome creation.

First Week: Be Green

Explore Interest Groups

Be sure that adult leaders are waiting when the first child arrives. Greet and welcome each child. Get the child involved in an activity that interests him or her and introduces the theme for the day's activities. Help nonreaders go to the activity designated for younger children.

Dish Gardens (For Younger Children)

- Give each child a plastic tub. (You may reuse clean, empty butter tubs.)

- Encourage the children to decorate the tubs with stickers.

- Fill a shallow dish with water.

- Fill a second shallow dish with alfalfa or grass seeds.

- Soak the sponge pieces in water.

- Show the children how to roll the wet sponges in the seeds.

- Help each child spread gravel on the bottom of the butter dish. Make sure the children keep the gravel away from ears, noses, and mouths.

- Have the children put a layer of sand on top of the gravel.

- Then instruct the children to put a layer of soil on top of the sand.

- **Say:** God created the rocks, sand, and soil we are using in our dish gardens.

- **Ask:** God created soils in different colors. They can be black, red, yellow, white, brown, and gray. What color soil are we using in our dish gardens?

- Show the children how to plant flower seeds or plants in the soil.

- Let the children place the seed-soaked sponges around the outer edges of the flowers.

- **Say:** God also created the seeds and plants we are using in our gardens. When we grow plants and grass, we are helping the soil. The plants and grass hold the soil down and keep it from eroding. Eroding means that the soil is washing or blowing away from the earth.

- Lightly water the dish garden. The grass seeds will sprout in a few days.

- **Say:** Our Bible verse is from the book of Psalms. The person who wrote the psalm is talking to God and saying, "You let us rule everything your hands have made" (Psalm 8:6, CEV). God wants us to rule over the earth. A good ruler, like a good king or queen, takes care of everyone and everything in his or her kingdom. When we grow plants we are being good rulers; we are taking care of the earth. We call a good ruler over the earth a good *steward*.

Prepare

- ✓ Provide: old newspapers; shallow plastic tubs; shallow dish; alfalfa or grass seed; flower seeds or small flower plants such as astrium or marigold; pea gravel; sand; soil; old sponges; scissors; stickers (left over from previously used curriculum); and water.
- ✓ Cover the table with old newspapers.
- ✓ Clean the old sponges by running them through a dishwasher without detergent. Cut the sponges into small pieces.

Make a Terrarium (for Elementary Children)

- Give each child 2 two-liter bottle bottoms.
- Have each child place pebbles in one of the bottoms.
- Add a layer of sand on top of the pebbles.
- Give each child a paper bag with a charcoal briquette in it. Let the child use a hammer to smash the briquette inside the bag.
- Pour the crushed briquettes on top of the sand.
- Put a layer of soil on top of the briquettes.
- **Ask:** God created soils in different colors. They can be black, red, yellow, white, brown, and gray. What color soil are we using in our terrariums?
- **Say:** It is important for us to keep soil clean and healthy. I wonder what we can do to keep soil clean and healthy.
- Plant small plants such as ivies, mosses, and ferns.
- **Say:** One thing we can do to help soil be clean and healthy is to grow plants. Plants hold the soil down and keep it from eroding. Eroding means that the soil is washing or blowing away.
- Water the plants lightly.
- Place the other bottle bottom on top to close the terrarium.
- **Say:** Our Bible verse is from the book of Psalms. The person who wrote the psalm is talking to God and saying, "You let us rule everything your hands have made" (Psalm 8:6, CEV). God wants us to rule over the earth. A good ruler, like a good king or queen, takes care of everyone and everything in his or her kingdom. When we grow plants we are being good rulers; we are taking care of the earth. We call a good ruler over the earth a good *steward.*

Tree Prints (for All Ages)

- Have the children wear smocks to protect their clothing.
- Give each child a piece of paper that has already been printed on one side. Show the children the printed side.
- **Say:** Today we will be using paper we have already used before. This side is printed, but if we turn it over there is a blank side we can use for painting. We are recycling our paper. That means we are using it again.
- Have the children turn their paper to the blank side.
- Show the children the natural items you have provided.
- Show the children how to make nature prints by pressing an item gently into the paint, then pressing the object onto the paper.

Prepare

- ✓ Provide: 2 two-liter bottles per child, craft knife, pebbles, sand, potting soil, charcoal briquettes (not quick lighting), small brown paper bags, hammer, mosses, ferns, ivies, and water.
- ✓ Adults only: Cut all the two-liter bottles in half with a craft knife.

Terrarium Tips

- ✓ Place the terrarium in indirect sunlight.
- ✓ If water droplets form on the outside of the terrarium there is too much water. Leave the top off for a day or two.
- ✓ Every few weeks check the soil in the terrarium to see if it is dry. If dry, add a small amount of water.

Prepare

- ✓ Cover the table with old newspapers.
- ✓ Provide: old newspapers; smocks; shallow pans; sponges; tempera paint; previously used paper; tree leaves, twigs, pine needles, and pine cones.
- ✓ Place a sponge in the shallow tray.
- ✓ Pour a small amount of paint on the sponge. Spread the paint out.

- **Say:** God created all these things to grow on trees. Trees help people live on the earth. Trees clean the air we breathe and help keep us cool. They provide food for us and for animals. They also provide homes for many different kinds of wildlife.

- **Ask:** What can we do to help trees? *(Plant more trees.)*

- **Say:** Isn't it amazing how God planned for trees? When we plant trees and take care of trees we are being good rulers; we are taking care of the earth. We call a good ruler over the earth a good *steward*. Being a good steward means that we are taking responsibility to care for the earth.

Earth Ball (For All Ages)

- Play this game with two or more players.

- Use masking tape to mark lines on the floor beginning about two feet from the basket. Place another line about one foot beyond the first line. Continue until you have a total of five lines, with the farthest about six feet from the basket. Each line represents a letter in the word EARTH.

- Let each child stand on the first line and try to make a basket. If the child makes the basket, he or she earns the letter E and draws a "Green Earth Fact." Help the child read the fact to the other children. Then instruct the child to go to the end of the line. On this child's next turn, he or she moves to the second line and tries to make a basket to earn the letter A.

- If the child does not make the basket, he or she does not get a letter or read an "Earth Fact." He or she moves to the back of the line and tries again to earn the letter E.

- Continue the game, moving farther away from the basket with each letter, until someone earns all the letters in the word EARTH.

Prepare

✓ Set up an empty box, trash can, or bucket in an open area of the room to be the basket.
✓ Provide: soft, squishy balls; masking tape; clean, empty can; and scissors.
✓ Photocopy and cut apart "Green Earth Facts" (page 24). Place the facts in a clean, empty can.

Play Practice (For All Ages)

- Invite children who enjoy participating in dramas to be part of "Creation Comes to Life."

- Assign roles to the children. Give the nonspeaking roles that represent each day of Creation to children who do not enjoy reading out loud. Assign one child or many children to be the voice of God. Assign an older child or an adult the narrator role.

- Children will enter the stage area before the beginning of their assigned day and kneel on the floor until their cues are read. The narrator and the voice of God can be off stage and out of sight.

- Practice reading the story and going through the motions. The children will present the play during large group time.

- You may want to videotape the children acting out the Creation story and then have everyone watch the video during large group time.

Prepare

✓ Photocopy "Creation Comes to Life" (pages 21–22) for the narrator and the voice of God.
✓ Cut the following props out of posterboard: one yellow circle (sun); one white circle (moon); and four yellow stars.
✓ Provide: flashlight; blue tablecloth; brown tablecloth; basket; silk flowers; silk leaves; and double-stick tape.
✓ Put double-stick tape on the back of each cutout.

Large Group

Bring all the children together to experience the Bible story. Blow a soda bottle shofar (see page 55) to alert the children that it is large group time. Use the transition activity to move the children from the interest groups to the large group area.

Earth Tag (Transition Activity)

- Signal large group time. Have the children stop what they are doing in their interest groups. Instruct the interest group leader to give the directions for Earth Tag.

- **Say:** We're going to play a game to move to our large group time. You will need to know today's Bible verse for the game. Let's say the Bible verse together: "You let us rule everything your hands have made" (Psalm 8:6, CEV). To play the game, everyone will wander around the room. Wandering with us will be someone holding an earth ball. If you are tagged with the ball, you must say today's Bible verse, then pick up a Bible, and finally sit down in front of the stage *(or whatever you call your large group area)*.

- Play Earth Tag with the children until everyone is seated.

- **Say:** Our Bible story is from the first book in the Bible, *Genesis.*

- Help the children find the first chapter of Genesis in their Bibles. Be sure to have older children or adults ready to help nonreaders.

- **Say:** Find the large 1. That's chapter one. What are the first three words right after the one? *(In the beginning)* Genesis means *beginning.* Chapter one tells us about the beginning of the world.

- Have the children place their Bibles on the floor beside them.

Hear, See, and Act the Story of Creation

- Lead the children in singing one or more of the recycle songs (pages 4–5).

- **Say:** Our God created an awesome universe. Let's see how it all began.

- Present "Creation Comes to Life."

- **Say:** God created every living thing. And that includes us. When God created humans, God gave us a big responsibility. We can find out what that was by looking in our Bibles.

- Have the children pick up their NRSV Bibles.

- **Say:** Find Genesis, chapter one again. That's the big number 1. Now find the little number twenty-six. Look at the words as I read the verse: "Then God said, 'Let us make humankind in our image, according to our likeness, and let them have dominion over the fish of the sea, and over the birds of the air, and over the cattle, and over all the wild animals of the earth, and over every creeping thing that creeps upon the earth'" (Genesis 1:26).

Prepare

- ✓ Recruit one or more leaders to hold an earth ball and tag the children.
- ✓ Provide an earth ball.
- ✓ Provide CEV Bibles. Place the Bibles where the children can easily access them.

Earth balls are available at Oriental Trading Co. 1-800-875-8480 or *www.orientaltrading.com*

Prepare

- ✓ Provide NRSV and CEV Bibles.
- ✓ Photocopy "Recycle Songs" (pages 4–5) for each child. Plan to reuse the song sheets for each lesson.

- **Ask:** What does the word *dominion* mean? *(to rule over)*

- **Say:** The word *dominion* reminds me of the word *rule*, and that reminds me of our Bible verse, Psalm 8:6. Let's have a race to see how fast you can find Psalm 8:6 in your Bible. If you want to come up front and be in the race, hold up your hand.

- Choose four to six children to come up front. They may bring CEV Bibles or you can give them Bibles when they are on stage.

- Pair the children in teams of two. If you have older and younger children, pair an older child with a younger child. Each pair needs a Bible.

- **Say:** When I say, "Go!" work together with your partner to find the verse. As soon as you find the verse, raise your hand. Are you ready? Find Psalm 8:6. Set. That's Psalm 8:6. Go!

- Encourage all the children to cheer as the partners work together to find the verse.

- Have the first pair to find the verse and raise their hands, read the verse.

- Thank the children who came to the front and have them sit down.

- **Ask:** So what is our big responsibility? *(to rule over everything God made)*

- *Say:* Let's think about some ways we can be good rulers over creation.

- Dismiss the children to their small groups.

Small Groups

Divide the children into small groups. You may organize the groups around age-levels or around readers and nonreaders. Keep the groups small, with a maximum of ten children in each group. You may need to have more than one of each group.

Young Children

- Settle the children in a group on the floor or around a table.

- Review the Creation story with the children.

- Give each child a napkin and a graham cracker.

- Let the children use the yogurt and gummy animals to depict an edible creation scene.

- Say a thank-you prayer and enjoy the treats.

- Give each child a piece of previously used paper and colored pencils.

- **Ask:** What is a caretaker? What are some things we can do to take care of God's creation? *(pick up litter, take care of pets, plant trees)*

- **Say:** We are going to learn about what it means to be a caretaker of God's creation. Use the colored pencils to draw a picture of something you can do to take care of God's creation.

- Encourage the children to show their finished pictures to the group.

Prepare

✓ Provide: reusable bowls, spoons, and napkins; graham crackers; vanilla yogurt; food coloring; and gummy animals.

✓ Scoop vanilla yogurt into several small bowls. Use food coloring to die the yogurt different colors such as blue, yellow, and green.

✓ Provide used paper and colored pencils.

✓ Photocopy "Good Steward Checklist" (page 23) for each child.

- Hold up the "Caretaker of God's Creation Covenant" (page 64).

- **Say:** This is a covenant. A covenant is a promise between God and us. When God created the earth, God gave people all the gifts of the earth. Then God told the people to be responsible for creation and to be good stewards of what we were given. In this covenant we promise to care for God's creation.

- Read the "Caretaker of God's Creation Covenant" (page 64). Have the children repeat each line after you.

- Give each child the "Good Steward Checklist" (page 23) to share with their families.

- Close with prayer.

Elementary Children

- Settle the children in a group on the floor or around a table.

- Read Genesis 1 from *The Message*.

- Give each child a graham cracker to use as an edible canvas.

- Let the children use the yogurt and gummy animals to depict an edible creation scene. Invite them to tell the group about their edible creations.

- Say a thank-you prayer and enjoy the treats.

- **Say:** God says that people are in charge of the earth of have dominion over creation. In *The Message*, the Bible I just read to you, God tells the people to "be responsible" for all living things.

- **Ask:** Has anyone every told you to "be responsible"? What did the person mean when you were told that? What do you think God is trying to tell people when God says it to people? What are some responsible ways we can take care of God's creation?

- Give each child a piece of used paper and some colored pencils. Have the children use the colored pencils to draw a picture of one way you can take care of God's creation.

- Encourage the children to show their finished pictures to the group.

- Hand out the "Caretaker of God's Creation Covenant" (page 64).

- **Say:** This is a covenant. A covenant is a promise between God and us. When God created the earth, God gave people all the gifts of the earth. Then God told the people to be responsible for creation and to be good stewards of what we were given. In this covenant we promise to care for God's creation.

- Read the covenant together. Collect the copies to reuse next week.

- Close with prayer.

- Give each child the "Good Steward Checklist" (page 23) to share with their families.

✓ **Note:** Save the children's pictures to use again in Week 6.

Prepare

✓ Provide *The Message* by Eugene Peterson.
✓ Provide: reusable bowls, spoons, and napkins; graham crackers; vanilla yogurt; food coloring; and gummy animals.
✓ Scoop vanilla yogurt into several small bowls. Use food coloring to die the yogurt different colors such as blue, yellow, and green.
✓ Provide used paper and colored pencils.
✓ Photocopy "Good Steward Checklist" (page 23) and "Caretakers of God's Creation Covenant" (page 64) for each child. Plan to reuse the covenant each week.
✓ **Note:** Save the children's pictures to use again in Week 6.

Second Week: Think Green

Explore Interest Groups

Be sure that adult leaders are waiting when the first child arrives. Greet and welcome each child. Get the child involved in an activity that interests him or her and introduces the theme for the day's activities. Help nonreaders go to the activity designated for younger children.

Green Print Shopping Bags (All Ages)

- Have each child wear a smock to protect his or her clothing.

- Give each child a cloth shopping bag.

- Have the child place the bag flat on the table. Place a piece of used cardboard or posterboard inside the bag.

- Have the children fold one hand into a fist. Show them how to dip the side of the fist into the paint and then press it onto the bag. This will make the foot of a footprint.

- Next show the child how to dip a thumb into the paint and then press the thumb at the top of the footprint to make the big toe. Use other fingers to make prints for the remaining toes.

- Let the children make more than one footprint on their bags.

- **Say:** The green footprints we are making remind me of the words "carbon footprint" or "ecological footprint." These two kinds of footprints are talking about the damage we do to the earth. Think about walking along the beach. When we walk on the wet sand, we can stop, look behind us, and see our footprints. The water from the ocean washes away the sandy footprints, but the earth cannot wash away things we do to harm it.

- **Ask:** Can you think of some ways we leave harmful footprints on the earth? Ways that we are hurting God's creation? *(throwing away too much trash, cutting down forests that are homes for animals, using too much water and electricity, polluting the air)* Can you guess what happens to animals like turtles, fish, and birds when they eat trash like plastic bags or plastic rings? *(They die.)*

- **Say:** *An average person makes about 4.5 pounds of garbage per day. More than half of that trash goes to landfills.* About 70,000 truckloads of garbage are sent to landfills in North America every day. Lined up bumper to bumper, over a year they would stretch halfway to the moon. That's too much trash! An easy way we can help the earth is by using cloth bags instead of plastic bags. When we think ahead and take reusable bags to use when we shop, we reduce how much trash we make. *Reduce* is an important word. When we reduce, we use less of something. When we reduce how much trash we make, we are helping God's world.

Prepare

✓ Provide: a plain, light-colored cloth shopping bag for each child, old newspapers, used cardboard or posterboard, green paint, shallow tray, smocks, and hand-washing supplies.
✓ Cover the table with old newspapers.
✓ Pour green paint into a shallow tray.

Cloth bags are available at: *www.orientaltrading.com www.conventiontotes.com*

Art: Brenda Gilliam
© 2010 Abingdon Press

Water Play (Young Children)

- Show the children the three different bowls of water you have prepared. Encourage the children to feel the water in each bowl.

- **Ask:** What do you feel? Which bowl of water do you think fish would want to swim in?

- **Say:** Clean water is important to God's world. Water covers about two-thirds of the earth, but not all of that water is drinkable. Only about three-tenths of one percent of the earth's water can be used by humans. Four out of every ten people in the world do not have clean water.

- Let the children enjoy playing in the water table. Encourage the children to dip and pour with the water bottles.

- **Ask:** Can you think of some ways to help save water? *(Turn off the water when you brush your teeth; take a shower instead of a bath; use reusable containers instead of water bottles.)*

- **Say:** When you do things like turning off the water when you brush your teeth, you save water. When you drink water from reusable cups instead of water bottles, you help keep the earth clean because billions of these bottles wind up in the trash. When we save water, we reduce how much water we use. Reduce is an important word. When we reduce, we use less of something. When we reduce how much water we use, we are helping God's world.

Water Works (Elementary Children)

- Have one or two children sit or stand near each bowl or pan of water.

- **Say:** Clean water is important to God's world. Water covers about two-thirds of the earth, but not all of that water is drinkable. Only about three-tenths of one percent of the earth's water can be used by humans. Four out of every ten people in the world do not have clean water. Let's do an experiment to find out what happens when oil gets into our water.

- Add ½ teaspoon of cooking oil into each pan of water.

- **Ask:** Does the oil mix with the water?

- Instruct the children to take turns blowing gently across the water to create wind.

- **Say:** I wonder what happens when it's a windy day.

- Have the children use the feathers to stir the oil and water.

- ***Ask:*** What happened to the feathers? What do you think happens to birds like ducks and geese when they land on oily water?

- Encourage the children to try to clean the oil out of the water with a cotton rag, a piece of old pantihose, and a paper towel. (You may need to add a little more oil for this part of the experiment.)

Prepare

✓ Provide: three bowls; water; cooking oil; dishwashing soap; towels; water table or large plastic tub; and clean, empty water bottles.

✓ Partially fill each bowl with water. Add ½ teaspoon cooking oil to one bowl, ½ teaspoon soap to the second bowl, and leave only water in the third bowl.

✓ Provide a water table or make a water play area by partially filling a plastic tub with water. Have towels nearby to dry hands and spills.

Prepare

✓ Provide a pie pan, cake pan, or bowl for every one or two children.

✓ Provide: ½ teaspoon measuring spoon, water, cooking oil, dishwashing soap, feathers, cotton rags, old pantihose cut into pieces, and paper towels.

✓ Partially fill each container with water.

✓ Provide towels to dry hands and spills.

- **Ask:** Which one worked the best? Were you able to clean up all the oil?

- Add ½ teaspoon of dishwashing soap.

- **Ask:** What happened to the oil? Is the water clean now?

- **Say:** No, the soap breaks up the oil but it doesn't get rid of the chemicals in the oil. Oil is just one of the things that pollutes our water. Other things include pesticides, fertilizers, and sewage. In the United States we dump sixteen tons of sewage into our waters each minute. That's over 23,000 tons of sewage each day!

- **Ask:** Can you think of some ways to help save water? *(Turn off the water when you brush your teeth; take a shower instead of a bath; use cleaners that don't hurt the earth.)*

- **Say:** When you do things like turning off the water when you brush your teeth, you save two gallons of water. That means we are reducing how much water we use. Reducing is an important word. When we reduce, we use less of something. When we reduce how much water we use, we are helping God's world.

Two Gallons Relay (All Ages)

- Have the children make at least two lines at the starting line. Have the same number of children in each line. If you have an uneven number of children, have the first child in the shorter line do the relay twice.

- **Say:** Today we are talking about the word *reduce*. When we reduce, we use less of something. We can help God's creation by reducing how much water we use. When you do things like turning off the water when you brush your teeth you save two gallons of water. Let's look at two gallons of water.

- Show the children the two gallons of water.

- **Say:** Let's have a relay race to carry the gallons of water. When I say, "Go!" the first person in line will pick up the two gallons of water and carry them around the chair and then back to the front of the line. The next person in line will then take the gallons of water and start the relay. Continue the relay until everyone in the line has a turn carrying the water gallons.

- Shout, "Go!" and start the relay.

- After the relay, instruct the children to sit down and rest.

- **Say:** Think about all the different ways you use water each day. Let's count the different ways.

- Encourage the children to think about different ways we use water, such as taking a bath or shower, swimming, washing dishes, washing clothes, watering plants, watering the lawn, playing in the sprinkler.

- **Ask:** Can you think of ways to save water? *(Take a shower instead of a bath; don't water the lawn every day; wash clothes and dishes only when you have a full load, and so forth.)*

Prepare

✓ Use an open area of the room.

✓ Make a starting line by taping masking tape across the floor.

✓ Place a chair across from the starting line to indicate the relay lane. Make the distance between the starting line and the chair appropriate for the ages of the children running the relay.

✓ Provide two clean gallon milk or juice jugs with handles for each relay lane. Fill the jugs with water and secure the lids.

✓ Place two gallon water jugs at the starting line of each relay lane.

Large Group

Bring all the children together to experience the Bible story. Blow a soda bottle shofar (see page 55) to alert the children to the large group time. Use the transition activity to move the children from the interest groups to the large group area.

Glue Tag (Transition Activity)

- Signal large group time. Have the children stop what they are doing in their interest groups. Instruct the interest group leader to give the directions for Glue Tag.

- **Say:** Let's play glue tag to gather everyone for large group time. *(Name of person)* will be IT. Whenever IT touches you, you must hold onto IT's waist and go everywhere that IT goes. Then IT and the person IT has tagged become IT and go after someone else. When that peron is tagged, he or she goes to the end of the line and holds onto the last person's waist. When the whole group is a part of the line the game is over. As the line gets longer, the persons who are a part of the line cannot let go, but they can help IT capture the last remaining persons by blocking their path or surrounding them.

- Give the children a few minutes to see how long it takes for IT to gather all the children into the line.

- Instruct IT to lead the children to the large group area and have everyone sit down.

- **Say:** The game wasn't over until everyone was included in the line. We are all part of God's plan for creation, every one of us.

Prepare

✓ Choose an adult leader or an older child to be IT. Explain the game to IT.

Hear, See, and Act the Story of Creation

- Lead the children in singing one or more of the recycle songs (pages 4–5).

- **Say:** Our Bible verse is Psalm 8:6. Let's race to find our verse. Who wants to come up front?

- Choose four to six children to come up front. They may bring their Bibles or you can give them Bibles when they are on stage.

- Pair the children in teams of two. If you have older and younger children, pair an older child with a younger child. Each pair needs a Bible.

- **Say:** When I say, "Go!" work together with your partner to find the verse. As soon as you find the verse, raise your hand. Are you ready? Find Psalm 8:6. Set. That's Psalm 8:6. Go!

- Encourage all the children to cheer as the partners work together to find the verse.

- Have the first pair to raise their hands, read the verse.

- Thank the children who came to the front and have them sit down.

- **Ask:** What is our big responsibility? *(to rule over everything God made)*

Prepare

✓ Provide CEV Bibles.
✓ Provide the "Recycle Songs" (pages 4–5) song sheets.

- **Say:** Our Bible story today is from the very first book in the Bible, the book of Genesis.

- Help all the children find the first chapter of Genesis in their Bibles. Be sure to have older children or adults ready to help nonreaders.

- **Say:** Find the large number 2. That's chapter two. Read verses one, two and three. The verses are the small numbers after the large 2.

- **Ask:** What did God do on the seventh day? *(God rested.)*

- Have the children place their Bibles on the floor beside them.

- **Say:** Listen as I retell the Creation story. Each time I say, "And God saw that…" I want you to say, **"it was good!"** and sign the word **good** in American Sign Language.
  Let's see, what has God done so far?
  God said, "Let there be light." And God saw that **it was good!**
  God said, "Let there be oceans." And God saw that **it was good!**
  God said, "Let there be plants." And God saw that **it was good!**
  God said, "Let there be a sun." And God saw that **it was good!**
  God said, "Let there be a moon and stars." And God saw that **it was good!**
  God said, "Let there be animals." And God saw that **it was good!**
  God said, "Let there be people." And God saw that **it was good!**

  God made a whole lot more. And that's what happened the first six days. God created and created and created. Then on the seventh day, God rested. God took time to enjoy God's creation. God decided rest was more than good, it was holy. So God said that the seventh day was a special day, a day for rest.

  God said, "Let there be rest." And God saw that…**it was good!**

  Based on material written by Virginia Kessen © 2006, 2009 Abingdon Press.

- **Say:** I wonder how God rested. Let's try a resting exercise.
  Lie down flat on your back on the floor.
  Extend your legs outward and relax your arms by your side.
  Close your eyes.
  Inhale and exhale three times.
  Tense the muscles in your feet. Relax the muscles.
  Tense the muscles in your legs. Relax the muscles.
  Now tense the muscles in your back and your stomach. Relax.
  Tense the muscles in your arms. Relax.
  Now tense the muscles in your fingers. Relax.
  Tense the muscles in your shoulders and in your neck. Relax.
  Tense the muscles in your face. Relax.
  Inhale and exhale three times.
  Breathe in and out as we pray.

- **Pray:** Thank you, God, for everything you have created, and thank you for a special day of rest. Help us know when to work and play, and when to rest. Amen.

- Quietly dismiss the children to their small groups.

Art: Robert S. Jones
© 1998 Abingdon Press

Good: Touch the fingers of the right hand to the lips. Move the hand down and place it palm up in the left hand.

Small Groups

Divide the children into small groups. You may organize the groups around age-levels or around readers and nonreaders. Keep the groups small with a maximum of ten children in each group. You may need to have more than one of each group.

Young Children

- Give each child a sheet of wax paper and ¼ cup play dough.

- **Say:** Let's review the story of Creation from Genesis chapter one.

- Have the children shape a number 1 with their play dough.

- **Say:** On the first day, God created light, day, and night. Quickly rework your play dough into a shape that reminds you of daytime. Now rework your dough into something that reminds you of night.

- Have the children shape a number 2.

- **Say:** On the second day, God created water and sky. Use half of the play dough to make waves of water. Use the other half to make clouds.

- Have the children shape a number 3.

- **Say:** On the third day, God created rivers, lakes, oceans, dry land, mountains, and all kinds of plants and trees. Quickly mound your dough into a tall mountain. Now use your dough to make a tree.

- Have the children shape a number 4.

- **Say:** On the fourth day, God created the sun, moon, and stars. Make either the sun, the moon or some stars with your play dough.

- Have the children shape a number 5.

- **Say:** On the fifth day, God created fish, other sea animals, and birds. Make either a fish or a bird.

- Have the children shape a number 6.

- **Say:** On the sixth day, God created land animals and people. Shape your dough into an animal or into the shape of a person.

- Have the children shape a number 7.

- **Ask:** What did God make on the seventh day? *(Nothing. God rested.)*

- **Say:** Nothing. God rested on the seventh day.

- Place each child's play dough in a resealable container to send home.

- Have the children wash their hands.

- **Say:** Our Bible tells us that God blessed the seventh day as a day of rest. The word we use to describe this day of rest is *sabbath*. The sabbath is a day when we can stop and think about God. It is also a day when we can stop and allow the earth to rest. I wonder what we can do to help the earth have a sabbath.

Prepare

- ✓ Purchase or make play dough. You will need ¼ cup, or about 2 ounces, for each child.
- ✓ Provide wax paper and crayons.
- ✓ **Note:** Do not encourage the children to share the play dough. Sharing play dough shares germs. Send the play dough home with each child in a resealable container to be used again.
- ✓ Photocopy "Help the Earth Rest" (page 25) for each child.

- Give each child a copy of "Help the Earth Rest" (page 25).

- Have the children place an X on the pictures that show ways we don't use the earth's resources wisely.

- Talk with the children about ways we can let the earth rest. These might include the ideas pictured on "Help the Earth Rest" as well as not watching television for one day or not using the car for one day.

- **Say:** All the things we talked about save energy. When we save energy, we are saving the earth's resources. We are giving the earth a rest.

- Turn "Help the Earth Rest" over. Let the children use crayons to draw a picture of something they can do to help the earth rest.

- Read the "Caretaker of God's Creation Covenant" (page 64). Have the children repeat each line after you.

- Close with prayer.

Elementary Children

- Give each child a copy of "What Does the Bible Say?"

- Encourage the children to look up these verses to see where the Bible talks about who rested and then match the Bible verse with the picture of the person who is resting.

- **Say:** The Bible tells us it is important for people to rest. It is also important for the earth to rest. Let's look up one more Bible verse, Genesis 2:1-3.

- Have the children look up and read the verses.

- **Say:** Our Bible tells us that God blessed the seventh day as a day of rest. The word we use to describe this day of rest is sabbath. The sabbath is a day when we can stop and think about God. It is also a day when we can stop and allow the earth to rest. I wonder what we can do to help the earth have a sabbath.

- Give each child a copy of "Help the Earth Rest" (page 25).

- Have the children place an X on the pictures that show ways we don't use the earth's resources wisely.

- Talk with the children about ways we can let the earth rest. These might include the ideas pictured on "Help the Earth Rest" as well as not watching television for one day or not using the car for one day.

- **Say:** All the things we talked about save energy. When we save energy, we are saving the earth's resources. We are giving the earth a rest.

- Turn "Help the Earth Rest" over. Let the children use crayons to draw a picture of something they can do to help the earth rest.

- Hand out the "Caretaker of God's Creation Covenant" (page 64).

- Read the covenant together. Collect the copies to reuse next week.

- Close with prayer.

Prepare

✓ Provide Bibles and crayons.
✓ Photocopy "Help the Earth Rest" and "What Does the Bible Say?" (page 25) for each child.
✓ Reuse "Caretaker of God's Creation Covenant" (page 64).

Creation Comes to Life

by Suzann Wade

Cast
God: One or more children (off stage voice).
Narrator: Adult or older child.

Nonspeaking Roles
Day One: One child with a flashlight.

Day Two: Two children with a blue tablecloth.

Day Three: One child with a blue tablecloth, one with a brown tablecloth, and one with a basket of flowers.

Day Four: Four children. One carries a large yellow circle for the sun, one carries a smaller white circle for the moon, and two others each carry two stars. The sun, the moon, and the stars all have double-stick tape on the back.

Day Five: Three children to act like fish. Two children to act like birds.

Day Six: Six children. Four will be animals and two, one boy and one girl, will be humans. The four children who are animals kneel in the front of the stage area. The other two children go to the back of the stage area and lie on the floor.

Adult: One adult to turn off and on the lights every evening and morning.

(Turn off all lights in the room. Day One enters and kneels on the floor. Day One has a large flashlight.)

Narrator: In the beginning, there was God. Out of nothing, God called everything into creation. God said . . .

God: Let there be light! *(Day One stands and turns on the flashlight.)*

Narrator: And there was light. Then God said . . .

God: Let there be dark! *(Turn off flashlight.)*

Narrator: And there was dark. Then God said . . .

God: This is GOOD!

Narrator: There was evening. And there was morning. *(Adult turns the room lights on.)* That was the first day.

(Day One exits. Day Two children enter and kneel.)

Narrator: Then God said . . .

God: Let there be a dome to divide the waters. *(Day Two children stand and raise the tablecloth between them.)*

Narrator: And God called the dome the sky. And God said . .

God: This is GOOD!

Narrator: There was evening. *(Adult turns the room lights off.)* And there was morning. *(Adult turns the room lights on.)* That was the second day.

(Day Two children exit and Day Three children enter. The child with the brown tablecloth wraps up in the tablecloth and kneels on the ground. The next child covers the first child with the blue tablecloth, then kneels to the side. The third child with the flowers kneels behind them both.)

Narrator: Then God said . . .

God: Let the waters come together and let the land appear. *(The first child stands and pulls the blue tablecloth to one side. The child wrapped in the brown tablecloth stands. The third child remains kneeling.)*

Narrator: God called the land, earth, and the waters, sea. Then God said . . .

God: Let there be plants and flowers. *(The third child stands and tosses plants and flowers around the stage area. The child with the brown tablecloth lays it on the floor.)*

Narrator: And God said . . .

God: This is GOOD!

Narrator: There was evening. *(Adult turns the room lights off.)* And there was morning. *(Adult turns the room lights on.)* That was the third day.

(Day Three children exit and Day Four children enter and kneel.)

Narrator: Then God said . . .

God: Let there be lights in the sky. *(Day Four children stand and hold up the sun, moon, and stars.)*

Narrator: God created the sun to warm the day. *(Child with the sun sticks it on the wall.)* God created the moon to light the night. *(Child with the moon sticks it on the wall.)* And God filled the sky with stars. *(Children with the stars stick them on the wall.)* And God said . . .

God: This is GOOD!

Narrator: There was evening. *(Adult turns the room lights off.)* And there was morning. *(Adult turns the room lights on.)* That was the fourth day.

(Day Four children exit and Day Five children enter and kneel.)

Narrator: Then God said . . .

God: Let there be fish and creatures to swim in the sea. *(Fish children stand and pretend to swim around the stage. They can make whale or dolphin noises, if they wish.)*

Narrator: And soon there were all kinds of fish and whales and dolphins filling the waters. Then God said . . .

God: Let there be birds to fill the air. *(Bird children stand and pretend to fly around the stage and make bird noises.)*

Narrator: And birds took flight and filled the skies. And God said . . .

God: This is GOOD!

Narrator: There was evening. *(Adult turns the room lights off.)* And there was morning. *(Adult turns the room lights on.)* That was the fifth day.

(Day Five children exit and Day Six children enter. The animal children kneel in the front of the stage. The humans lie down at the back of the stage.)

Narrator: Then God said . . .

God: Let there be animals to fill the earth. *(Animal children stand and begin moving around the stage and making noises like different animals.)*

Narrator: And all kinds of animals began to move around the earth. Then God said . . .

God: Now, let's make people. The people will be like God, both the girls and the boys will be like God, to think and act and love like God.

Narrator: So, God created humans. *(Children in the back, stand and stretch and rub their eyes.)* Then God said . . .

God: I want to show you all that I have created. *(All the children from all the days come back on stage. The humans walk around looking at all the parts of creation.)* I am putting you in charge of my creation. Take care of it and provide for it. *(Humans act as if they are feeding and petting the animals, fish, and birds or watering the flowers.)*

Narrator: God looked at all of creation. God was very pleased and God said . . .

God: This is VERY GOOD!

Narrator: There was evening. *(Adult turns the room lights off.)* And there was morning. *(Adult turns the room lights on.)* That was the sixth day.

(All the children from all the days stay on stage and lie down on the floor.)

Narrator: On the seventh day, God rested. God created the seventh day as a day of rest so that all people can take time to remember God and the glory of creation. There was evening. *(Adult turns the room lights off.)* And there was morning. *(Adult turns the room lights on.)* And that is how it all began.

© 2004 Abingdon Press

Green Church

Good Steward
Checklist

(Circle One)

I recycle newspaper.	Yes	No
I turn off the water when I brush my teeth.	Yes	No
I use both sides of paper.	Yes	No
I recycle glass, plastic, and aluminum.	Yes	No
I turn off lights when I leave the room.	Yes	No
I reuse paper bags.	Yes	No
I do not waste food.	Yes	No
I walk or ride my bicycle instead of riding in a car for short trips.	Yes	No
I take short showers.	Yes	No
I treat animals with respect.	Yes	No

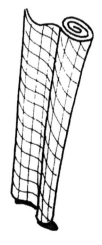

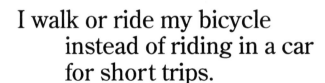

Art: Megan Jeffery © 1999 Abingdon Press

Green Earth Facts

Garbage in a landfill lasts for about thirty years.

Each person throws away about four pounds of garbage a day.

One bus carries as many people as forty cars.

One-third of all water is used to flush the toilet.

Each one of us uses about twelve thousand gallons of water every year.

About five million tons of oil wind up in the ocean each year.

We dump fourteen billion pounds of trash into the ocean every year.

Recycling one ton of paper saves seventeen trees.

It takes plastic five hundred years to break down.

Eighty-four percent of what we throw away at home can be recycled.

One million sea birds are killed each year because of eating plastic.

We use five billion aluminum cans each year.

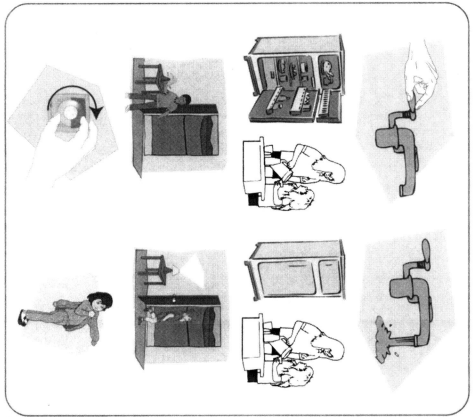

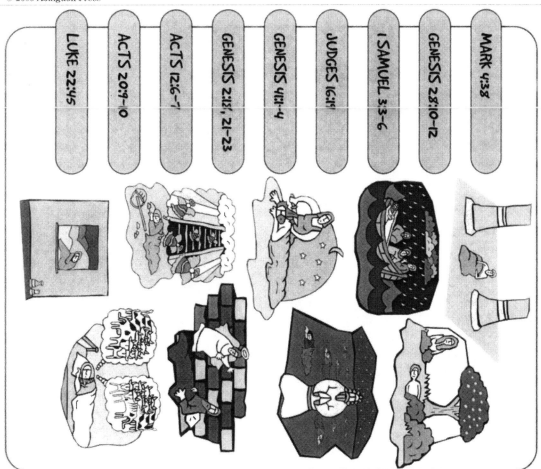

LUKE 22:45

ACTS 20:9-10

ACTS 12:6-7

GENESIS 2:1-2, 21-23

GENESIS 41:1-4

JUDGES 16:19

1 SAMUEL 3:3-6

GENESIS 28:10-12

MARK 4:38

Lesson 1: In the Beginning

 # In the Garden
Act Green • Live Green

Objectives

The children will
• hear Genesis 2:4-23;
• recognize that God wants us to be good stewards of creation;
• learn that being a good steward means to take personal responsibility for taking care of the earth;
• experience ways to take care of creation.

Bible Story

Genesis 2:4-23: the creation of Adam and Eve as the first human beings.

Bible Verse

Psalm 8:6, CEV: You let us rule everything your hands have made.

Focus for the Teacher

Two Stories of Creation

There are actually two Creation stories in the Book of Genesis. In the first story (Genesis 1:1—2:4), God speaks the world into being over six days. The second Creation story (Genesis 2:5:—4:26), focuses not on a God who creates with mighty commands, but on one who nurtures from the dust the creature, man, with whom God chooses to be in relationship.

> ## You let us rule everything your hands have made.
>
> **Psalm 8:6, CEV**

Feeling that man should not be alone, God creates woman, Eve, which means "living." Together they complete the creation; one helps the other.

God places the humans in the garden of Eden. We can imagine what the garden must have been like—lush, beautiful, peaceful, and containing everything needed for a long and happy life.

Psalm 8:6, CEV

The Bible in These Lessons

Genesis 2:4-23

In a very descriptive passage, God forms man, Adam, from dust. The word "man" is translated from the Hebrew word *adam*, which can also be translated "humankind." God breathes into the human the very breath of life. The Hebrew word for "soul" is derived from the same root word as "breath." God is literally breathing the soul into the first human and makes him a unique living creature with special responsibilities. The man was given specific instructions to till the ground and tend the plants.

We are continuing with Psalm 8:6 for the Bible verse: "You let us rule everything your hands have made." This verse is a reminder of our responsibility to be caretakers of the earth.

About the Children

This story emphasizes God's loving and caring nature. Younger and older children need to know that they are not the results of random acts of science. Of all the living things that God created, only humans can plan, choose, remember, pray, worship, imagine, and create.

Third Week: Act Green

Explore Interest Groups

Be sure that adult leaders are waiting when the first child arrives. Greet and welcome each child. Get the child involved in an activity that interests him or her and introduces the theme for the day's activities.

Garden Planter (For All Ages)

- **Say:** Today our Bible story is from the second chapter of Genesis. It tells about God creating Adam and Eve in the Garden of Eden. When God created Adam, God told Adam to take care of the garden. Let's make a planter that will take care of watering itself.

- Have the child thread the string through the bottle cap.

- Instruct the child to screw the lid onto the bottle, leaving some of the string hanging out of the cap and some of the string inside the bottle top.

- Have the child place the top upside down inside the bottom of the bottle.

- Let the child fill the top with potting soil and then plant a small plant in the soil.

- Have the child remove the bottle top with the plant and ask a friend to hold it so that he or she can fill the bottom of the bottle about half full of water.

- Place the top upside-down in the bottom with the string dangling in the water. The string will act like a wick to move water into the soil.

Prepare

✓ Provide clean two-liter plastic bottles. You may have one bottle for each child or make two or three bottles to use in the room.

✓ Cut the top one-third off each bottle.

✓ Drill a hole in each cap.

✓ Cut string into 12-inch lengths.

✓ Provide: potting soil, small plants, and old newspapers.

✓ Cover the table with old newspapers.

Garden Paper (For All Ages)

- Help the children follow these directions:
  1. Put ¼ cup of cotton linter into a bottle half filled with water.
  2. Tear about a two-inch square from colorful tissue paper scraps. Then tear the square into pieces, ¼ inch or smaller.
  3. Add the tissue pieces and 10 to 12 flower seeds to the water.
  4. Important: Screw the lid *securely* onto the bottle.
  5. Shake the bottle for a minute or two until the pulp is mixed well.
  6. Place a plastic canvas square on top of a bowl with a cookie cutter on top.
  7. Carefully pour pulp to the edges of the cookie cutter shape.
  8. Gently push the pulp to the edges of the cookie cutter so it is evenly distributed.
  9. Remove the cookie cutter.
  10. Turn the canvas upside down on several layers of paper towel.
  11. Gently remove the plastic canvas.
  12. To grow flowers, place the seed paper onto soil and water it daily.

Prepare

✓ Provide: cotton linter; scraps of colored tissue paper; clean, empty 16-oz water bottles with tops; water; flower seeds; cookie cutters; plastic canvas; bowls; recycled paper towels.

✓ Cover the table with old newspapers.

✓ *Note:* Cotton linter is available at craft stores or on the web at:

www.enasco.com or
www.fineartstore.com

- **Ask:** We are reusing several things to make our garden paper. What are they? *(tissue paper scraps, water bottles, cookie cutters)*

- **Say:** We are using recycled paper towels. If every household in the United States replaced one roll of non-recycled paper towels with a roll of recycled paper towels, we would save 864,000 trees.

- **Say:** When we reuse things, we are being good stewards.

- **Ask:** What does being a good steward mean? *(We take care of God's world.)* Why do you think it is important to reuse things? Why don't we just throw things away and use all new things? *(It makes less trash to reuse things; it costs more money.)*

Garden Homes for the Birds (For All Ages)

- Give each child a milk or juice carton with the holes already cut.

- Show each child how to insert a short dowel or twig in the smaller hole to make a perch.

- Have the child close the top of his or her carton and then glue the top shut.

- Encourage the children to decorate the outside of the cartons with things from nature. This could include leaves, twigs, bark, moss, or dried flower petals.

- When the glue is dry, poke a hole in the top of the carton and attach a loop of wire or string to make a hanger.

- **Ask:** What usually comes in these cartons? What do you do with the cartons when you have finished the juice or milk?

- **Say:** The amount of wood and paper we throw away each year is enough to heat fifty million homes for twenty years. Instead of throwing these cartons away, we have reused them to make something that will help God's world. We have made shelters, or homes, for the birds. Reusing things is one way we can be good stewards.

Garden Games (For All Ages)

- **Say:** Today our Bible story is from the second chapter of Genesis. It tells about God creating Adam and Eve in the Garden of Eden, so we have several Garden Games for you to choose to play. Each of these games are made from things that are reusable. When we reuse materials instead of just throwing them away, we are keeping trash out of landfills.

- **Note:** These games may be played inside or outside.

Can Stilts

- Let the children decorate the cans with pieces of colored tape.

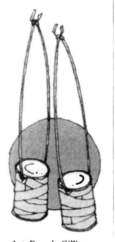

Art: Brenda Gilliam
© 2010 Abingdon Press

Prepare

✓ Provide clean, empty milk or juice cartons. The cartons can be a variety of sizes.

✓ Cut a 1½ inch round hole 3 inches above the bottom on one side of each carton. This will make the entrance for the birds.

✓ Poke a smaller hole below the entrance hole for the perch.

✓ Gather leaves, twigs, bark, moss, and dried flower petals.

✓ Provide short dowels or twigs, glue, and wire or string.

Prepare

✓ Provide: two clean coffee cans, hand-held can opener with triangular end, rope or clothesline, scissors, and colored electrical or duct tape.

✓ Turn the cans upside down so that the open end is facing the floor. Use the can opener to punch two holes on either side of each can near the bottom end.

✓ Cut two lengths of rope or clothesline about 72-inches long. Thread a rope through the holes in each can. Tie the two ends of each rope together into a loop. This will make the handles.

- Have the children take turns standing on the cans and holding the ropes taut. Let the children try to walk on the stilts.
- **Note:** Provide adult supervision.
- **Ask:** What usually comes in these cans? What can we do with these cans besides throw them away? *(Reuse them; recycle them.)*

Golf

- Let the children decorate the coffee cans by gluing on scraps of construction paper or tissue paper.
- Lay the coffee cans on their sides in an open area of the room to make a mini golf course. The cans will become the holes.
- Number each hole by placing a piece of used paper on the floor next to the can. Write the number on the paper.
- Let the children take turns using the toy golf clubs to hit plastic golf balls into the cans.
- **Ask:** What usually comes in these cans? What can we do with these cans besides throw them away? *(Reuse them; recycle them.)*
- **Say:** Reusing cans keeps them out of landfills. Most garbage is buried in landfill sites, but the amount of land that can be used for landfills is running out. Eighty percent of all the trash we throw away could be recycled and reused. Instead of throwing these cans away we have reused them. Reusing things is one way we can be good stewards.

Bowling

- Set up the bottle bowling pins in an open area of the room.
- Let the children take turns rolling a ball to knock down the pins.
- **Say:** We throw away 2.5 million plastic bottles every hour.
- **Ask:** What are some ways we can reuse plastic bottles? *(Refill them with water or juice; use them for games and crafts.)* What are some things we can do to not use plastic bottles at all? *(Put our drinking water in refillable containers.)* When we reuse things we would usually throw away, we are good stewards.

Toss and Catch

- Let the children decorate the milk jugs with the colored tape.
- Have the children make a ball by rolling up a used plastic bag and wrapping the bag with tape.
- Encourage the children to take turns using the scoops to toss and catch the ball.
- **Ask:** What usually comes in these jugs? Millions of plastic milk jugs are thrown away each year. What can we do with these jugs besides throw them away? *(Reuse them; recycle them.)*

Prepare

✓ Provide several clean coffee cans or powdered drink cans. They can be a variety of sizes.

✓ Provide: scraps of construction paper or tissue paper, glue, used paper, toy golf clubs, and plastic golf balls.

Prepare

✓ Provide: ten clean, empty 2-liter plastic bottles; a rubber ball; and masking tape.

✓ Pour about an inch of sand into the bottom of each bottle. Tightly screw on the cap.

✓ Mark a bowling lane with strips of masking tape.

Prepare

✓ Provide two clean plastic milk jugs.

✓ Use sharp scissors or a utility knife to cut off the bottom of the milk jug. Then cut a U shape under the handle to make a scoop. (Do not cut into the handle.)

✓ Provide colored electrical tape or duct tape and used plastic shopping bags.

Large Group

Bring all the children together to experience the Bible story. Blow a soda bottle shofar (see page 55) to alert the children to the large group time. Use the transition activity to move the children from the interest groups to the large group area.

Reuse Relay (Transition Activity)

- Signal large group time.

- Have the children stop what they are doing in their interest groups and get ready to move to large group time.

- Instruct the interest group leader to give the directions for Reuse Relay.

- **Say:** We're going to play a relay game to move to our large group time. Let's line up for our teams.

- Instruct the children to line up in at least two teams in the large group area, opposite from the Reuse and Trash boxes. Make sure the space in between is clear of any obstacles.

- Place a box full of trash behind each team of children.

- Instruct the first child in line to reach into the box behind him or her and pull out a piece of trash. The team must decide if it is something that can be reused or something that must be thrown away.

- Once they make their decision, the first child must run the length of the room, place the item in the Reuse or Trash box, and then run back to tag the next child in line.

- The game continues until one team empties its box.

- Have the children sit down in the large group area, facing the stage.

- *Say:* How much of the trash in your team's box was reusable?

Hear, See, and Act the Story of Creation

- Lead the children in singing one or more of the recycle songs (pages 4–5).

- **Say:** Our Bible story is from the second chapter of Genesis. God made light for day and night. God made plants and trees and flowers to grow upon the earth. God created all kinds of animals to live in the sky, in the sea, and on the earth. But creation wasn't finished.

  God wondered, "Who will enjoy all the good things I have created? Who will take care of the earth? Who will take care of the animals?

  "No one," thought God. "No one."

  So God created people. First God created Adam—a human being, a man, made in God's image. God formed Adam from the dust of the earth. God breathed life into Adam and he became a living being. Then God planted a beautiful garden called "Eden." Two trees—the

Prepare

✓ Place two large boxes on one side of the room opposite the large group area. Mark one box "Reuse" and the other box "Trash."

✓ Provide a box for each team. Fill each box with clean trash. Make sure some of the items are reusable or recyclable. You need to have as many items as you have children on each team.

Prepare

✓ Provide CEV Bibles.

✓ Provide the "Recycle Songs" (pages 4–5) song sheets.

Tree of Life and the Tree of the Knowledge of Good and Evil—grew in the middle of the garden. God placed the man in the garden and said, "You may eat the fruit of any tree, except one. Never eat fruit from the Tree of the Knowledge of Good and Evil."

Then God saw that even with all the wonderful plants and animals in the garden, Adam was still alone. The man didn't have anyone to talk to.

So God created Eve, the woman. This woman was created in God's image as well. Then God blessed the man and woman and told them, "You will be the keepers of my garden."

God looked around. Now everything was as it should be. The sun gave light to the day. The moon and stars gave light to the night. Plants and flowers and trees bloomed in the garden. Creatures of of every sort swam in the sea, flew in the sky, and moved on the land. And there were people—people who could know and love God. People who could care for God's creation. It was very good.

Adapted from Exploring Faith™: Middle Elementary, Student, Fall 2000. Written by LeeDell Stickler. © 2000 Cokesbury.

- Hand out the Bibles to the children.

- *Say:* Find Genesis, chapter two. That's the big number 2. Now find the little number 15. Look at the words as I read the verse: "The LORD God put the man in the Garden of Eden to take care of it and to look after it" (Genesis 2:15, CEV).

- *Say:* In our Bible story God put Adam in the Garden of Eden to take care of it. Our Bible verse tells us to take care of the earth. Let's race to find our verse. Who wants to come up front?

- Choose four to six children to come up front. They may bring their Bibles or you can give them Bibles when they are on stage.

- Pair the children in teams of two. If you have older and younger children, pair an older child with a younger child. Each pair needs a Bible.

- Say: When I say, "Go!" work together with your partner to find the verse. As soon as you find the verse, raise your hand. Are you ready? Find Psalm 8:6. Set. That's Psalm 8:6. Go!

- Encourage all the children to cheer as the partners work together to find the verse.

- Have the first pair to raise their hands, read the verse.

- Thank the children who came to the front and have them sit down.

- **Ask:** What is our big responsibility? *(to rule over everything God made)*

- Dismiss the children to their small groups.

Small Groups

Divide the children into small groups. You may organize the groups around age-levels or around readers and nonreaders. Keep the groups small, with a maximum of ten children in each group. You may need to have more than one of each group.

Young Children

- **Say:** At the very beginning when God created the world, God also created a wonderful garden. The most delicious fruits and vegetables grew in this garden. Let's make a Garden of Eden fruit salad for a snack.

- Let the children empty the canned fruit into a large mixing bowl. Do not drain.

- Slice the banana into the bowl.

- Choose a child to sprinkle the dry pudding mix over the fruit.

- Have the children take turns stirring the mixture until there are no lumps.

- Leave the empty fruit cans, pudding box, and banana peel out on the table.

- Serve the fruit salad in small reusable bowls.

- Say a thank-you prayer and enjoy eating the fruit.

- Tell the children the story, "The Gift of the Buffalo" (page 41).

- **Ask:** What are some of the things we throw away when we cook and eat a meal? *(cartons, plastic bags, cardboard boxes, foam trays, plastic containers, aluminum cans, food, and so forth)*

- Point out the leftover cans, packages, and banana peel to the children.

- **Ask:** What do you think the Native Americans who honored the gift of the buffalo would say about the amount of this trash? What lesson can we learn from their use of the buffalo?

- Encourage the children to find ways to reuse the cans, box, and peel. *(puppets, pencil holders, compost, posters about caring for the earth, and so forth)*

- Let the children use the art supplies to make one or two of their suggestions. If they choose to make posters, display the posters around the church.

- Read the "Caretaker of God's Creation Covenant" (page 64). Have the children repeat each line after you.

- Close with prayer.

Prepare

- ✓ Provide ingredients and utensils for Garden of Eden Fruit Salad (see below).

- ✓ Provide: reusable bowls, spoons, and napkins.

- ✓ Provide: art supplies such as posterboard, glue, crayons or markers, scraps of paper, and yarn.

Garden of Eden Fruit Salad

- ✓ one 16-ounce can of pineapple chunks

- ✓ one banana

- ✓ one small can of mandarin orange sections

- ✓ a small box of instant lemon pudding mix

- ✓ large mixing bowl

- ✓ can opener

- ✓ knife

- ✓ large mixing spoon

Note: This recipe serves six to eight children.

Elementary Children

- Settle the children in a group on the floor or around a table.

- Give each child a reusable bowl, spoon and cloth napkin.

- Without offering an explanation to the children, set a large mixing bowl containing the Garden of Eden fruit salad between two children sitting next to each other. Then set a small bowl with some of the fruit salad in the center for the remaining children.

- Let the children work out the problem of the uneven distribution themselves. Encourage them to seek a solution, but do not tell them what they should do.

- When the children have found a solution for the problem, let them discuss the activity.

- **Say:** What happened when I handed out the snack? Did I give everyone a fair share of the snack? What did you all do with the snack? Why? Why do you think I gave out the snack the way I did?

- Show the "World Resources Pie Chart" (page 41) to the children.

- **Ask:** This is a pie chart. Why do you think it is called a pie chart? Have you ever shared a pie with other people? How would you feel if one person took almost all of the pie and just left a tiny slice for everyone else?

- **Say:** Resources are the supplies needed for all types of things such as fuel, food, electricity, heat, clothes, and almost everything you own. This chart shows how the world's resources are divided. See how just a couple of people get the biggest piece and most of the people have to share the little piece?

  The people with the biggest piece represent North America and Europe. Only twenty percent of all the people in the world live in North America and Europe. However, the people in North America and Europe use eighty-six percent of the world's resources. The other eighty percent of the people in the world live in other places. They use fourteen percent of the world's resources.

  So, those of us who live in places like North American and Europe can help the rest of the people in the world by reducing the amount of energy we use and the amount of waste we produce. One way we can reduce our waste and use less energy is to reuse as many things as we can. That's why we used bowls and spoons that we can wash and use again for today's snack.

- **Ask:** What else can we reuse? *(cloth napkins, dish towels, outgrown clothes, books, games, and toys, cloth shopping bags, and so forth)*

- Hand out the "Caretaker of God's Creation Covenant" (page 64).

- Read the covenant together. Collect the copies to reuse next week.

- Close with prayer.

Prepare

- ✓ Provide ingredients and utensils for Garden of Eden Fruit Salad.

- ✓ Provide: reusable bowls, spoons, and napkins.

- ✓ Provide: art supplies such as posterboard, glue, crayons or markers, and scraps of paper, and yarn.

Garden of Eden Fruit Salad

- ✓ Ingredients: one 16-ounce can of pineapple chunks, one banana, one small can of mandarin orange sections, a small box of instant lemon pudding mix.

- ✓ Utensils: large mixing bowl, can opener, knife, large mixing spoon, one large and one small serving bowl, two serving spoons.

- ✓ Empty the canned fruit into a large mixing bowl. Do not drain. Slice the banana into the bowl. Sprinkle the dry pudding mix over the fruit. Stir the mixture until there are no lumps. Serves six to eight children.

- ✓ Place most of the fruit salad in one large bowl. Place the remaining fruit salad in a small bowl.

- ✓ Reuse the "Caretaker of God's Creation Covenant" (page 64).

fourth Week: Live Green

Explore Interest Groups

Be sure that adult leaders are waiting when the first child arrives. Greet and welcome each child. Get each child involved in an activity that interests him or her and introduces the theme for the day's activities. Help nonreaders go to the activity designated for younger children.

Recycled creations (All Ages)

- Show the children the trash.

- **Say:** Every day, the average American produces a little more than four pounds of trash. That's enough to fill over 63,000 trash trucks. If everyone in the world produced as much trash as we do, then we would need two more planets just to hold all the trash.

- **Ask:** Where does all this trash go? *(landfills, dumps, into the ocean)*

- **Say:** Much of our trash goes into landfills. Making more and more landfills destroys the homes of hundreds of animals. Recycling is a wonderful way to reduce the amount of trash we make and reduce the negative impact we have on the land and the animals of the earth.

- Read Genesis 2:18-20 to the children.

- **Say:** After God created Adam, he also created birds and animals. God brought the animals to Adam to name.

- Set out the art supplies.

- **Say:** You may use any of these supplies and any of this trash to create an animal. After you create your animal, give it a name.

- Let the children use their imaginations to create animals (real or imaginary) using the trash and art supplies.

- Encourage the children to share their animals' names.

- Display the animals around the classroom or church.

Prepare

- ✓ Provide a Bible.

- ✓ Provide clean, unbreakable trash, such as: egg cartons, boxes, plastic bottles, plastic bags, newspapers, fast food containers, and so forth.

- ✓ Provide art supplies, such as: glue; paint; tape; crayons or markers; and scraps of colored paper, fabric, and yarn.

- ✓ Cover the table with old newspapers.

Recycle center (Younger children)

- **Ask:** What are some ways that we can take care of God's world? *(pick up litter, care for pets, turn off electricity when it is not in use, feed the birds, turn off the water while brushing teeth, recycle, and so forth)*

- **Say:** Those are good suggestions. When we do things like pick up litter and care for pets we are taking care of God's world and being good stewards. Recycling is another way we can be good stewards.

- Show the children the wrapped box (see page 35).

Prepare

- ✓ Provide items for a recycle box, such as: a large box, paper bags, glue, crayons or markers, paper scraps, used plastic lids, plastic rings from six-packs of soda or water, and used cardboard.

- **Say:** When we find a new use for something that was going to be trash, we are recycling. Instead of throwing this big box away, let's use it to collect things that can be recycled.

- Explain that you reused paper bags to wrap the box.

- Point out the "Recycle Here" list on the box.

- Encourage the children to decorate the box by gluing on the recyclable items you have provided.

- Help the children place the box where parents and other church members will see it.

- Give each child a "Recycle Here" (page 43) list.

- Have the children decorate the back of the list with crayons or markers.

- **Say:** Let's recycle things from home. Have your moms and dads read the list to see what things they can bring for our recycle box.

Prepare

- ✓ Cut open the paper bags and use the paper to wrap the box.

- ✓ Photocopy "Recycle Here" (page 43) for each child plus one to glue on the box.

- ✓ Glue one copy of "Recycle Here" to the box.

Crushing for Creation (for Elementary Children)

- Encourage the children work in groups of two to three children to create pyramids or towers out of aluminum cans that can be recycled.

- Let the groups show off their creations.

- Optional: take pictures of the teams with their structures. Use the pictures to create a poster promoting recycling.

- Have the teams designate one child as the can handler. Give that child a pair of work gloves.

- Give each team a piece of cardboard and have them place the cardboard on the floor.

- Instruct the can handler to place one or two cans in the center of the cardboard.

- Let the children crush the cans.

- Have the can handler pick up the crushed cans and put them in a recycling box.

- **Ask:** What is recycling? What happens when you recycle something? *(New products are made.)*

- **Say:** New products are made from the recycled materials, such as new aluminum cans or plastic or glass bottles. Recycled paper products can be made from recycled newspapers and paper. Recycling also saves energy. The same amount of energy is used to make one aluminum can from scratch as is used to make twenty aluminum cans from recycled aluminum.

- **Ask:** What happens to all the plastics, bottles, and paper if we don't recycle? *(It goes into landfills as trash.)*

Prepare

- ✓ Provide clean, empty aluminum cans.

- ✓ Provide work gloves and a piece of cardboard for each team.

Turtle Races (For All Ages)

- Give each child two thin paper plates.

- Encourage the children to use markers to decorate the backs of the paper plates to be turtle shells.

- Show each child how to stack the two paper plates on top of one another so that the decorated sides are to the outside.

- Help each child tape around the edges of the two paper plates, leaving a section open.

- Let the children stuff the turtle backs with crumpled newspaper.

- Help each child tape the open section closed.

- Have the children move to an open area of the room for turtle races.

- Use masking tape on the floor to mark a starting line.

- Use masking tape on the floor to mark a finish line. This should be several feet from the starting line.

- Have each child lie on his or her stomach at the starting line.

- Place a turtle back on each child's back.

- Shout, "Go!" and let the children crawl like a turtle on their stomachs to the finish line. The children must keep their shells on their backs. If the turtle shell falls off, the child must go back to the starting line. The first child to the finish line still wearing his or her shell wins the race.

- If you have a large number of children participating, form relay lines for the race. Start the first child in each line, allow some space, and then start the next group.

- **Say:** God wants us to take care of the earth. That means taking care of animals. One way we can help animals is by not using or by recycling plastic bags. Plastic bags are a problem for sea turtles. When plastic bags get into the ocean, they look like jelly fish, sea turtles' favorite food. When a sea turtle eats one, the bag gets stuck in the turtle's stomach and makes the turtle think it isn't hungry. Then the turtle dies of starvation. Tens of thousands of whales, birds, seals, and turtles are killed every year by plastic bag litter.

Prepare

✓ Provide: two thin paper plates per child, markers, masking tape, and used newspapers.

Recycling Commercials (For All Ages)

- Encourage the children to create commercials about how recycling helps the earth and the animals on the earth.

- Have the children practice the commercials so they are ready to perform the commercials for large group time.

- Let the children use old hair brushes, socks, cereal boxes, or paper bags to make puppets that become the stars in the commercials.

Prepare

✓ Provide: old hair brushes, socks, cereal boxes, or paper bags.

✓ Provide art supplies, such as: glue; tape; feathers; crayons or markers; and scraps of colored paper, fabric, and yarn.

Large Group

Bring all the children together to experience the Bible story. Blow a soda bottle shofar (see page 55) to alert the children to the large group time. Use the transition activity to move the children from the interest groups to the large group area.

Pick It Up (Transition Activity)

- Signal large group time.

- Have the children stop what they are doing in their interest groups and get ready to move to large group time.

- Instruct the interest group leader to give the directions for "Pick It Up."

- **Say:** Let's play "Pick It Up" to gather everyone for large group time. Choose a partner.

- Have the children choose partners. If you have an uneven number of children in your interest group, partner with one of the children yourself.

- Point out the trash that is scattered in the large group area.

- **Say:** When (name of leader) shouts, "Pick It Up!" move with your partner to one piece of trash on the floor. Listen to (name of leader). He or she will call out a body part. Then work with your partner to pick up the trash and take it to the recycling box—but you can only use that body part.

- When the leader shouts "Pick It Up!" encourage the partners to stand by a piece of trash.

- When the leader calls out a body part (elbow to elbow, foot to foot, knee to knee, knee to elbow, hand to foot, and so forth) encourage the partners to pick up the trash and move to the recycle box.

- Continue the game until all the trash is placed in the recycle box.

- Have the children sit down in the large group area.

Prepare

✓ Place a recycle box near the front of the large group area. This could be the box made by the younger children during the interest group time.

✓ Space out clean recyclable trash (newspaper, plastic bottles, food boxes, and so forth) on the floor. You will need at least one piece of trash per child.

✓ Choose an adult to be the leader.

Hear, See, and Act the Story of Creation

- Lead the children in singing one or more of the recycle songs (pages 4–5).

- **Say:** Look at the person next to you. Tell him or her the answers to the following questions.

- **Ask:** What's your name? How did you get your name? Did it come from a relative or friend? Did it come from someone important or famous? Did your parents make it up? Does it mean something special? Do you have a nickname? What is it?

- **Say:** Today's Bible story talks about names. Throughout the Creation story God creates and then gives creation a name—Day and Night, Sky, Sea, Earth, Sun, Moon, Stars. But in today's story, God turns the naming over to human beings.

Prepare

✓ Provide CEV Bibles.

✓ Provide the "Recycle Songs" (pages 4–5) song sheets.

- Tell the children the story "The Naming" (see page 42). Invite the children to supply the animal names.

- If you had an interest group preparing commercials, have the children present one commercial now.

- Hand out the Bibles to the children.

- **Say:** Find Genesis, chapter two. That's the big number 2. Now find the little number 19. Look at the words as I read the verse: "So the LORD took some soil and made animals and birds. He brought them to the man to see what names he would give each of them. Then the man named the tame animals and the birds and the wild animals. That's how they got their names" (Genesis 2:19-20, CEV).

- **Ask:** Giving a name to a creature gives it an identity. How do you think it felt to be given the responsibility to name all of the animals and birds? What are some ways we can take care of the animals and birds? *(feed them, take care of the earth so they have homes and food, keep them from becoming extinct)*

- **Say:** Some animals have become endangered because of things humans do to the earth. Endangered means that only a few of that kind of animal are alive. One way we can help endangered animals is to protect their homes. When we recycle, we are keeping things like plastic out of the water and off the land where it can harm animals. You will learn more about recycling to help animals in your small groups.

- **Say:** Our Bible verse is Psalm 8:6. Let's race to find our verse. Who wants to come up front?

- Choose four to six children to come up front. They may bring their Bibles or you may give them Bibles when they are on stage.

- Pair the children in teams of two. If you have older and younger children, pair an older child with a younger child. Each pair needs a Bible.

- **Say:** When I say, "Go!" work together with your partner to find the verse. As soon as you find the verse, raise your hand. Are you ready? Find Psalm 8:6. Set. That's Psalm 8:6. Go!

- Encourage all the children to cheer as the partners work together to find the verse.

- Have the first pair to raise their hands, read the verse.

- Thank the children who came to the front and have them sit down.

- **Ask:** What is our big responsibility? *(to rule over everything God made)*

- If you had an interest group preparing commercials, have the children present the remaining commercials now.

- Dismiss the children to their small groups.

Small Groups

Divide the children into small groups. You may organize the groups around age-levels or around readers and nonreaders. Keep the groups small, with a maximum of ten children in each group. You may need to have more than one of each group.

Young Children

- Play "Endangered Animal Charades" with the children.

- **Say:** God had Adam name all the animals. I have a bag filled with animal names. Draw a name and look at it, but keep the name a secret from everyone else.

- Have each child draw a slip of paper from the bowl or bag. Whisper the name of the animal to any children who cannot read.

- Let the children take turns acting out the animal named on the paper.

- Encourage the children to guess the animal's name.

- **Ask:** All these animals have something in common. Can you guess what it is?

- **Say:** All these animals are endangered. Endangered means that only a few of that kind of animal are alive. One of the reasons animals become endangered is because of the trash humans make. A little bit of trash can make a huge impact on animals. Plastic bags and plastic rings like this one (Hold up the plastic rings from a six pack of soda or bottled water.) kill many turtles and seals and fish each year. These animals get plastic rings like these stuck in their mouths. Or they swallow the plastic bags and the bags get stuck in their stomachs. You may think it is no big deal when you see litter like this, but this plastic ring could still be here three hundred years from now. So a ring like this that somebody throws away can be a danger for years.

  Sometimes, even when we throw trash away properly, the trash gets scattered by animals or the weather. When you throw away rings like this, take the time to cut each of the rings apart so that it won't be a danger to animals.

- Use the scissors to cut all the rings apart.

- **Say:** When we take the time to do things like cutting these rings apart, we are taking responsibility for the fish and birds and animals. We are being good stewards of the earth.

- **Say:** What are some other ways we can be good stewards? *(pick up litter, care for pets, turn off electricity when it is not in use, and so forth)*

- Read the "Caretaker of God's Creation Covenant" (page 64). Have the children repeat each line after you.

- Close with prayer.

Prepare

- ✓ Photocopy and cut apart the "Endangered Animal Charades" (page 44).

- ✓ Place the names inside a reusable bowl or cloth bag.

- ✓ Provide scissors and plastic rings from six-packs of soda or water.

Elementary Children

- Give each child a rubber band.

- **Say:** Today we will see how just a little bit of trash can make a huge impact on animals. Place the rubber band around your little finger. Stretch the rubber band behind your hand and hook the other end on your thumb. Now without using your other hand, try to take the rubber band off.

- **Ask:** How hard is it to get the rubber band off?

- Collect the rubber bands.

- Hold up the plastic rings from a six-pack of soda or bottled water.

- **Say:** Many turtles and seals and fish are killed each year because they get plastic rings like these stuck in their mouths. You may think it is no big deal when you see litter like this, but this plastic ring could still be here three hundred years from now. Sometimes, even when we throw trash away properly, the trash gets scattered by animals or the weather. When you throw away rings like this, take time to cut the rings apart so that they won't be a danger to wildlife.

- Use the scissors to cut all the rings apart.

- **Say:** When we take the time to do things like cutting these rings apart, we are taking responsibility for the fish and birds and animals. We are being good stewards of the earth.

- **Ask:** What are some other ways we can be good stewards? *(pick up litter, care for pets, recycle, reuse, and so forth)*

- **Say:** One way we can be good stewards is to write letters. You can write letters to a company that is polluting the earth. You can write letters to the newspaper. You can even write letters to the President of the United States. Your letter might ask the company to stop polluting, or tell the newspaper how important it is to recycle, or tell the President to make laws that help endangered animals.

- Give each child a a piece of paper.

- Help the children think through who they want to send the letter to and what they want to say.

- Have the children write their letters.

- Have the children turn the letter over to the blank side.

- Encourage the children to draw a picture of a turtle or other animal on the back of the letter.

- Collect the letters. Be sure to follow through and mail the letters.

- Give each child a copy of the "Caretaker of God's Creation Covenant."

- Read the covenant with the children. Collect the copies to use again.

- Close with prayer.

Prepare

✓ Provide: rubber bands, paper, pens or pencils, crayons or markers, scissors, and plastic rings from six-packs of soda or water.

✓ Reuse the "Caretaker of God's Creation Covenant" (page 64).

Send letters to:

President _____

The White House

1600 Pennsylvania Avenue NW

Washington, DC 20500

Senator_____

U.S. Senate

Washington, DC 20510

Representative _____

U.S. House of Representatives

Washington, DC 20515

To find your state's senators and representatives, go to:

www.senate.gov

or

www.house.gov

The Gift of the Buffalo

by Suzann Wade

There are many different tribes of Native American people. Arapaho, Apache, and Cheyenne are among the tribes known as the Plains Indians because they lived on the northern, central, and southern plains of the United States. While these tribes are all different, all of them depended heavily on the buffalo to survive. Even though they killed buffalo, they saw the life of the buffalo as sacred. They honored and respected the gift of the buffalo.

For this reason, Native Americans only hunted and killed as many buffalo as they needed at a time. The buffalo was their primary source of meat and supplies.

When a buffalo was killed, every part of it was used in some way. No part went to waste. Tribes ate as much of the fresh meat as they could. The rest of the meat was dried in the sun to make jerky and saved for times when they could not hunt.

The hide or skin of the buffalo was used to make many things: tipis, clothes, blankets, moccasins, drums, and bedding. Small bones became tools, such as needles. Large bones were bound together to make sleds. The hair was used as yarn for sewing. Hooves were ground up to make glue. Horns were used to carry water or gunpowder. Hollow internal organs were dried in the sun and used as vessels.

The buffalo was seen as a gift that had been given to all the people. For this reason, every part of it was treasured and nothing was wasted.

World Resources Pie chart

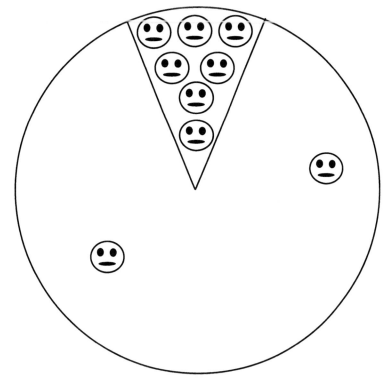

The Naming

by LeeDell Stickler

Long ago when the world was brand new,
God gave Adam a job to do.
"Since none of my creatures is ever the same,
I think it is time that each had a name."

So Adam invited the creatures to come.
Over the mountains and deserts, they came, one
by one.
Hopping and running and swimming they came.
And Adam gave each creature its very own name.
So listen as I tell you about each tail, foot, and nose,
And try to decide which name Adam chose.

This creature has four legs and a long, bushy,
striped tail. Its body is covered with thick fur. It
looks like a bandit because it is always wearing a
mask. I think I will call it _____.
(raccoon)

This creature has four legs and lives in a family
group called a pride. It has a long mane and a very
loud roar. I think I will call it _____.
(lion)

This creature has four legs and lives in the forests. It
has thick fur and a long nose. It likes to eat honey
and climb trees. I think I will call it
_____. *(bear)*

This creature has no legs but can move very fast. It
eats small animals. It makes a rattling sound to warn
you to "beware." I think I will call it
_____. *(rattlesnake)*

This creature has no legs at all and lives in the sea.
It looks like a fish but it has lungs and breathes air.
This creature is one of the largest creatures God
ever created. I think I will call it _____.
(whale)

This creature has only two legs. Its body is covered
with bright feathers—red, blue, green, and yellow.
This creature lives high in the trees of the tropical
rainforest. I think I will call it _____. *(parrot)*

This creature has four legs and carries its house
around on its back. It eats leaves and bugs. It moves
very slowly. I think I will call it _____. *(turtle)*

This creature has four legs and lives on the plains. It
has a very long neck so that it can reach the topmost
leaves of trees. This creature has brown spots on its
body. I think I will call it _____. *(giraffe)*

This creature has eight legs and lives in water. Its
favorite home is in the ocean near a coral reef. This
creature moves about by squirting jets of water. I
think I will call it _____. *(octopus)*

This creature has two legs and lives in caves and
dark attics. It's covered with fur and it flies. It makes
a high-pitched squeaking sound to locate objects. It
drinks the nectar of some plants and eats primarily
insects. This creature sleeps during the day and flies
around at night. I think I will call it _____.
(bat)

And so this is how each creature that is
Came by a name that is hers or his.

© 1997 Abingdon Press

Recycle Here

Recycle Here!

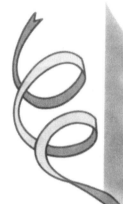

- paper towel rolls
- wrapping paper rolls
- tissue boxes
- unused or **saved gift wrap**
- ribbons
- yarn
- fabric scraps
- old pantyhose (washed!)
- cardboard egg cartons
- buttons

Help take care of God's earth by **recycling**! Our class will be using some everyday items from your home for **craft projects**. Here are some items that you can **recycle** by bringing them to the church to be used in the children's classes.

Endangered Animals

Blue Whale	Giant Panda	African Elephant	Golden Frog
Platypus	Red Wolf	Whooping Crane	Snow Leopard
Yellow-Throated Marten	Monk Seal	Jaguar	Sea Turtle
African Penguin	Amazon Pink River Dolphin	Polar Bear	Tiger

Green Church

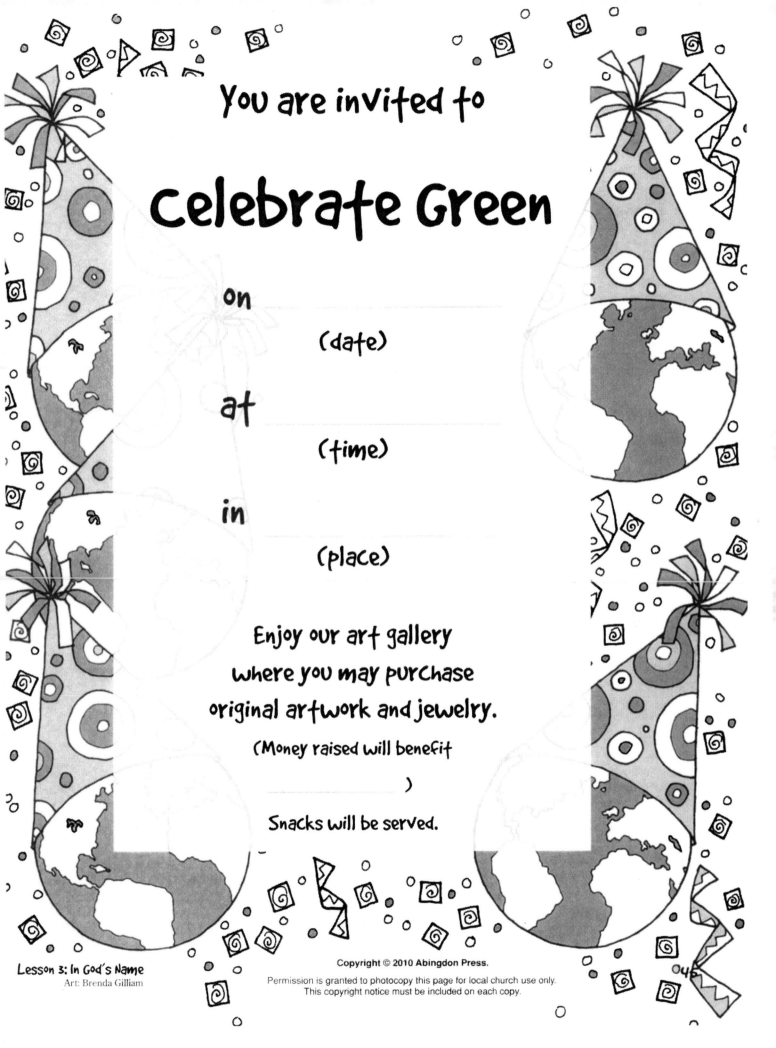

You are invited to

Celebrate Green

on _____

(date)

at _____

(time)

in _____

(place)

Enjoy our art gallery
where you may purchase
original artwork and jewelry.

(Money raised will benefit

_____)

Snacks will be served.

In God's Name
turn Green • Celebrate Green

Objectives
The children will
- hear Psalm 148;
- recognize that God wants us to be good stewards of creation;
- learn that being a good steward means to take personal responsibility for taking care of the earth;
- experience ways to take care of creation.

Bible Story
Psalm 148: This psalm calls on all creation—the heavens, the earth, the elements, all the animals, and people—to praise God.

Bible Verse
Psalm 8:6, CEV: You let us rule everything your hands have made.

Focus for the Teacher

All Creation Praises God

All creation praises God? Does this sound a little outrageous? How can a mountain praise God? How about the moon and the stars? And sea monsters? All creation praises God by being and doing exactly what God created it to do.

The Bible in these Lessons

Psalm 148
This psalm speaks poetically, but it tells about the greatness of God and the way God's creation praises the Creator. The first six verses call on the heavens to praise God. Not only are the angels called to worship, but also the sun, moon, stars, and clouds. This simply means that when the sun comes up each morning, when the moon and stars shine at night, it is a praise to the God who established the universe.

The next six verses call on the earth to praise God. The earth praises God by continuing to reproduce what God first made. The weather, the plants that grow and flourish, and all varieties of animals declare the greatness of God. People in all their variety are also a praise to God.

> You let us rule everything your hands have made.
>
> Psalm 8:6, CEV

The last two verses give reasons that we should choose to praise God. We should praise the Lord because God alone is exalted and God's glory is above heaven and earth. God has lifted us up and chosen us from all the creations in the world. We are held close to God's heart, like a loving parent holds a child. God loves us, and we love God. That is why we praise the Lord.

Psalm 8:6, CEV
We are continuing with Psalm 8:6 for the Bible verse: "You let us rule everything your hands have made." This verse is a reminder of our responsibility to be caretakers of the earth.

Plan a Celebration

Work with the children to plan a Green Celebration for Week 6. Photocopy the invitation (page 45) and send it home in Week 5. You may combine the celebration with fundraisers by selling the children's art work and necklaces. Let the children help plan where the money is donated. Several organizations that take care of the earth are listed on page 63.

Fifth Week: Turn Green

Explore Interest Groups

Be sure that adult leaders are waiting when the first child arrives. Greet and welcome each child. Get the child involved in an activity that interests him or her and introduces the theme for the day's activities.

Green Art Gallery (All Ages)

- Plan an art gallery with the children. Explain that the art they make will be on display for others to enjoy.

- **Say:** We're going to have a celebration next week. This week we will prepare the art gallery and make frames for pictures we will make next week. We want our art gallery to be green.

- **Ask:** What do you think we mean when we say we want our art gallery to be green?

- **Say:** This time the word *green* doesn't mean the color. It means that our art gallery will use things that show how much we care for the earth.

- Encourage the children to prepare frames for the art they will make in Week 6.

- Give each child a piece of cardboard. Help the child punch two holes in each corner of the cardboard.

- Show the child how to thread a piece of string or wire through the two holes at each corner from the back of the cardboard so that the ends of the string or wire are out.

- Instruct the children to place the cardboard flat on the table.

- Have each child cut or break sticks so that they are slightly longer than the sides of the cardboard.

- Show the child how to place the sticks on each edge of the cardboard, overlapping at the corners.

- Encourage the children to help each other by working in pairs. Have one child hold the sticks in place as the second child ties the sticks with the string or wraps them with the wire. This will make a natural wood frame.

- Set the frames in a safe place to use next week.

- Make plans with the children to sell the art work that will hang in the Green Art Gallery. The money raised could be used for an all-church green project or be sent to a group that is caring for the earth (See page 63).

Prepare

✓ Provide: small sticks or leaves, glue, and chenille stems.

✓ Cut cardboard pieces one inch larger on all sides than the Bible verse. Use the sides of boxes or other used cardboard.

✓ Cut four pieces of string, wire, or chenille sticks into four-inch lengths for each child.

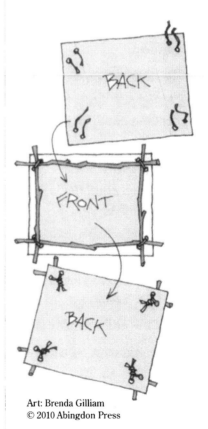

Art: Brenda Gilliam
© 2010 Abingdon Press

Green Crayons (for Younger Children)

- Have the children remove the papers from old, broken crayons.

- Let the children break the crayons into small pieces.

- Place the crayons into muffin tins. Children may use all the same color, or they can combine crayons to create new colors.

- Place the muffin tins in the oven until the crayons melt (5 to 10 minutes).

- Remove the tins from the oven and allow to cool. You can place the muffin tin in the freezer to make the cooling go faster.

- Pop the new crayons out of the tins.

- Save the crayons to use in Week 6.

- **Say:** This is a good way to reuse these old crayons. When we reuse things, we say we are being green. Good stewards like to be green. Next week, we'll use the crayons to make pictures to sell in our art gallery. We'll use the money we raise to help the earth. (Explain the project you have chosen.)

- **Ask:** Why don't we just throw things away and use all new things? *(It makes less trash to reuse things.)*

Green Necklaces (for Elementary Children)

- Let the children make paper bead necklaces from old wrapping paper or magazines. The children could sell the necklaces and donate the money to an organization that helps care for the earth (see page 63).

- Give each child a triangle pattern (page 63). Have the children cut out the pattern.

- Let the children go through the magazines and tear out colorful pages. Or let the children choose gently used gift-wrapping paper.

- Instruct the children to trace the triangle pattern onto the paper.

- Have the children cut out their triangles. Each child will need about twenty triangles.

- Instruct each child to place a paper triangle flat on the table with the color side facing up.

- Have the child use a sponge brush to spread glue onto the triangle.

- Have the child turn over the triangle. Beginning with the wide end, roll the triangle around a straw. Continue rolling until you reach the small point of the triangle.

- Instruct the child to slide the bead off the straw.

- Have the children repeat the process with each bead.

- Let the beads dry at least one hour.

- Tell the children that they will use the beads to make necklaces the next time they come.

- ✓ Preheat an oven to 300 degrees.
- ✓ Cover the table with old newspapers.
- ✓ Provide old, broken crayons and muffin tins.

Prepare

- ✓ Provide: used magazines or gift-wrapping paper; pencils; white glue; sponge brushes, drinking straws; and scissors.
- ✓ Photocopy the triangle pattern (page 63) for each child.

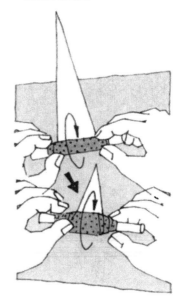

Green Ball (For All Ages)

- Play this game outside or in an open area of the room.

- **Say:** We're going to play catch, but we're going to make it green.

- **Ask:** What do you think we mean?

- **Say:** This time the word *green* doesn't mean the color. It means that our ball game will use things we can reuse or recycle.

- Divide the children into two groups. Give each group a cloth towel.

- Show the children the aluminum foil pieces. Have the children crumple the pieces together to form a ball.

- Instruct the children to use the towels to toss the ball back and forth between the two groups. See which group can toss the ball the highest, or how many times a group can catch the ball without missing.

Prepare

✓ Provide a cloth towel for each group.
✓ Provide clean, previously used aluminum foil.

Green Cleaners (For All Ages)

- Give each child a copy of "Danger Signs."

- Have the children match the signs to their meanings. Talk about any signs the children do not recognize.

- **Say:** These signs help us know when something is dangerous, poisonous, or harmful. Many cleaners we buy have chemicals that are dangerous to us and harmful to the earth. One of these chemicals is phosphate. Phosphates help get our clothes clean, but when this chemical gets into waste water it makes algae, a plant that grows in the water. Too much algae can kill fish and plants that live in the water. So what can we do? We can use natural products to make cleaners that are safe for the earth.

- Have the children smell the small container of vinegar.

- **Say:** We can use this vinegar to make a safe cleaner. It smells strong right now, but when it dries, the smell will disappear.

- Choose a child to pour vinegar into a spray bottle until it is half full. You may want to use a funnel. Help younger children as they pour.

- Choose another child to fill the bottle with water.

- Secure the lid. Let the children take turns shaking the bottle to mix the water and vinegar together.

- Provide an old t-shirt. Let the children take turns tearing the t-shirt into rags. You may want to cut the beginning of the tear with scissors.

- **Say:** Next week is our last lesson and we will end with a celebration. Let's clean our classroom to get ready for a celebration. Of course, we will use the safe cleaner we made and reusable rags.

- Let the children take turns using a rag and the cleaner to clean the windows or tables in your classroom.

Prepare

✓ Provide: white vinegar, water, a small container, a clean spray bottle, an old t-shirt, scissors, and a funnel.
✓ Photocopy "Danger Signs" (page 62) for each child.
✓ Pour white vinegar into a small container.
✓ Option: Provide a small spray bottle for each child and let him or her make a window cleaner to take home.

Large Group

Bring all the children together to experience the Bible story. Blow a soda bottle shofar (see page 55) to alert the children to the large group time. Use the transition activity to move the children from the interest groups to the large group area.

Step Up to Recycle (Transition Activity)

- Signal large group time.

- Have the children stop what they are doing in their interest groups and get ready to move to large group time.

- Have the interest group leader give each child two newspaper sheets.

- Instruct the interest group leader to give the directions for "Step Up to Recycle."

- Each child will race to the front of the large group area, stepping only on her or his newspapers.

- The child will lay one of the newspapers on the floor and step on it. Then the child will lay the other newspaper in front of him or her and step on it.

- The child will keep going forward, moving and stepping on the newspapers.

- When a child reaches the front of the large group area, have the child place the newspapers in a recycling bin and sit down, facing the stage.

- **Say:** We have been learning how important it is to recycle and reuse everyday things like newspapers. If every person in the United States recycled just one tenth of their newspapers, it would save about 25 million trees in a year.

Prepare

✓ Provide two sheets of used newspaper for each child.

✓ Place a recycle bin at the front of the large group area.

Hear, See, and Act the Story of Creation

- Lead the children in singing one or more of the recycle songs (pages 4–5).

- **Say:** A tone poem is a piece of music which tells a story or paints a picture using words. We're going to turn our Bible verse into a tone poem.

- Assign a different sound to each word in the Bible verse. Here are some suggestions, but encourage the children to come up with their own ideas.

  You: ahhh (expressing awe)
  let us: me, me, me (like a singer warming up)
  rule: clap hands once
  everything: make a windy, whistling noise
  your hands: snap fingers
  have made: pound one fist on top of the other

- Write each word and sound on a large piece of paper.

- Say the Bible verse together and make the sound after each word.

Prepare

✓ Provide: CEV Bibles, a large sheet of paper, and markers.

✓ Provide the "Recycle Songs" (pages 4–5) song sheets.

- Say the Bible verse again. This time encourage the children to say the words in their minds as you say them out loud. Have the children make the sounds after you say each word.

- Next time around, just use the sounds without speaking.

- **Say:** Our Bible verse reminds us that we are the caretakers for God's creation. Our Bible story is from Psalm 148. It is a song of praise for God, the Creator. In fact, the psalmist, the person who wrote the psalm, tells each part of creation to praise God. This story has a verse that repeats:

  Praise the name of the Lord.
  Praise the name of the Lord
  All Creation jump on board.
  And praise the name of the Lord.

  Each time you hear the verse, say it with me. On the word "jump," jump as high as you can.

- Read "Creation's Song of Praise" (page 61) to the children. Encourage them to jump and say the repeating chorus with you.

- Hand out the Bibles to the children.

- **Say:** Find Psalm 148. Now find the little number thirteen. Look at the words as I read the verse: "All creation, come praise the name of the LORD. Praise his name alone. The glory of God is greater than heaven and earth" (Psalm 148:13, CEV).

- **Ask** Why does the psalmist think creation should praise God? *(God is greater than heaven and earth.)*

- **Say:** Our Bible verse tells us to take care of the earth. Let's race to find our verse. Who wants to come up front?

- Choose four to six children to come up front. They may bring their Bibles or you can give them Bibles when they are on stage.

- Pair the children in teams of two. If you have older and younger children, pair an older child with a younger child. Each pair needs a Bible.

- **Say:** When I say, "Go!" work together with your partner to find the verse. As soon as you find the verse, raise your hand. Are you ready? Find Psalm 8:6. Set. That's Psalm 8:6. Go!

- Encourage all the children to cheer as the partners work together to find the verse.

- Have the first pair to raise their hands, read the verse.

- Thank the children who came to the front and have them sit down.

- **Ask:** What is our big responsibility? *(to rule over everything God made)*

- Dismiss the children to their small groups.

Small Groups

Divide the children into small groups. You may organize the groups around age-levels or around readers and nonreaders. Keep the groups small with a maximum of ten children in each group. You may need to have more than one of each group.

Young Children

- **Say:** The Native Americans view nature as something to be respected, not conquered. When native Americans of the Great Plains would hunt bison, they would use the entire animal, not just the meat. They would use the bones to make tools and the animal hides for clothing and shelter. They didn't believe in being wasteful with the blessings found on the earth.

- Show the children the bag.

- Walk around the room and allow each child to take one piece of chocolate.

- Invite the children to eat the candy.

- **Ask:** What should we do with the candy wrappers?

- If the children come up with ways to reuse the foil wrappers, then congratulate them on their ingenuity. If they want to throw the wrappers away, ask them what the Native Americans might have done.

- **Say:** Let's show respect for God and our planet by making a musical instrument with these leftover materials.

- Give the children a few minutes to brainstorm what instrument could be made from the leftovers. Challenge them to use only the leftover materials without adding any new ones.

- **Ask:** What about the bag?

- Some instrument examples include:
  1. Tear two pieces from the paper bag and rub them together.
  2. Crinkle the paper bag or the foil wrappers over and over.
  3. Roll several of the foil wrappers into balls and put them in the bag. Seal the open end of the bag and shake the balls inside to create a rattle.
  4. Blow up the paper bag. Form the foil wrappers into two sticks and tap the bag like a drum.

- Let the children take turns playing the instrument as you read Psalm 148 from a Bible. Collect the instrument to use again next week.

- **Say:** People are God's creation. One way we can show our praise to God is by taking care of the earth.

- Read the "Caretaker of God's Creation Covenant" (see page 64). Have the children repeat each line after you.

- Send home the invitation to next week's "Green Celebration" (page 45).

- Close with prayer.

Prepare

✓ Provide a Bible.

✓ Place one foil-wrapped chocolate piece (such as Hershey's Kisses®)for each child inside a lunch-sized paper bag.

✓ Check for allergies. If a child is allergic to chocolate, offer an appropriate substitute.

✓ Photocopy the "Green Celebration" invitation (page 45) for each child.

Elementary Children

- **Say:** The Native Americans are highly regarded for how they treat the earth. They view nature as something to be respected, not conquered. When native Americans of the Great Plains would hunt bison, they would use the entire animal, not just the meat. They would use the bones to make tools and the animal hides for clothing and shelter. They didn't believe in being wasteful with the blessings found on the earth.

- Show the children the bag.

- Walk around the room and allow each child to take one piece of chocolate. (If a child is allergic to chocolate, offer an appropriate substitute.)

- Invite the children to eat the candy.

- **Ask:** What should we do with the candy wrappers?

- If the children come up with ways to reuse the foil wrappers, then congratulate them on their ingenuity. If they want to throw the wrappers away, ask them what the Native Americans might have done.

- **Say:** Let's show respect for God and our planet by making a musical instrument with these leftover materials.

- Give the children a few minutes to brainstorm what instrument could be made from the leftovers. Challenge them to use only the leftover materials without adding any new ones.

- **Ask:** What about the bag?

- Some instrument examples include:
  1. Tear two medium-sized pieces from the paper bag and rub them together.
  2. Crinkle the paper bag or the foil wrappers over and over.
  3. Roll several of the foil wrappers into balls and put them in the bag. Seal the open end of the bag and shake the balls inside to create a rattle.
  4. Blow up the paper bag. Form the foil wrappers into two sticks and tap the bag like a drum.

- Let the children take turns playing the instrument as you read Psalm 148 from a Bible. Collect the instrument to use next week.

- **Say:** People are God's creation. One way we can show our praise to God is by taking care of the earth.

- Hand out the "Caretaker of God's Creation Covenant" (see page 64).

- Read the covenant together. Collect the copies to reuse next week.

- Send home the invitation to next week's "Green Celebration" (page 45).

- Close with prayer.

Prepare

- ✓ Provide a Bible.

- ✓ Place one foil-wrapped chocolate piece (such as Hershey's Kisses®) for each child inside a lunch-sized paper bag.

- ✓ Check for allergies. If a child is allergic to chocolate, offer an appropriate substitute.

- ✓ Photocopy the "Green Celebration" invitation (page 45) for each child.

- ✓ Reuse the "Caretaker of God's Creation Covenant" (page 64).

Sixth Week: Celebrate Green

Explore Interest Groups

Be sure that adult leaders are waiting when the first child arrives. Greet and welcome each child. Get the child involved in an activity that interests him or her and introduces the theme for the day's activities. Help nonreaders go to the activity designated for younger children.

Celebrate with a Green Art Gallery (For All Children)

- Give the children the recycled crayons they made in Week 5 and previously used paper.

- Encourage the children to use the recycled crayons to draw something they have learned about caring for the earth.

- Give the children the frames they made in Week 5 (see page 47).

- Have them glue the picture in the center of the cardboard.

- Attach a piece of wire or string as a hanger.

- Display the pictures in a hallway or on bulletin boards to make a "Green Art Gallery."

Prepare
✓ Provide; the recycled crayons made in Week 5, and previously used paper.

✓ Provide the frames made in Week 5 (see page 47).

Celebrate With Green Necklaces (For Elementary Children)

- Give the children the beads made in Week 5 (see page 48).

- Help the children cut string or dental floss into 32-inch lengths.

- Have the children thread the beads onto the string or floss.

- Help the children tie the ends of the string or floss together in a double knot.

- If you have decided to sell the necklaces, display them for sale.

Prepare
✓ Provide: dental floss or string, and the beads made in Week 5 (see page 48).

Celebrate With Green Refreshments (For All Ages)

- Let the children prepare compost cups for the celebration.

- Have the children spoon chocolate pudding into reusable bowls.

- Let each child crumble a chocolate sandwich cookie and spread the crumbs over the pudding.

- Give each child one or two gummy worms to add to the bowl.

- **Say:** Our snack reminds me of dirt and composting. About thirty percent of all garbage is made up of waste from food and yards. Composting is a great way to recycle this kind of waste. It is a biological process that occurs when tiny microscopic organisms break down old plant

Prepare
✓ Provide reusable bowls and spoons.

✓ Provide: chocolate pudding, chocolate sandwich cookies, and gummy worms.

and animal tissues and recycle them to make new, healthy soil. Worms help this process by digging and eating some of the things in the dirt. Some of the things you can put in a compost pile are meat scraps, bones, milk, cheese, ice cream and oily foods. The new dirt made from composting is great for gardens.

- Save the compost cups for the celebration.

Celebrate With Green Instruments (For All Ages)

- **Say:** Today our Bible story is Psalm 148. It is a song of praise. We're going to make some musical instruments to play as we listen to the psalm. We will make all these instruments from things we can reuse and recycle. When we reuse things, we say we are being green. We are being good stewards. Americans throw away 2.5 million plastic bottles every hour. Instead of throwing these bottles away, we will use them to make some "green" instruments.

Clip Clop Hooves (For Younger Children)

- Give each child the bottom of two plastic bottles.

- Help the child use electrical tape to cover the cut edges of the bottles.

- Show the children how to use a hard flat surface, such as a table, on which to tape the open ends of the clip-clop hooves.

- **Say:** This instrument uses only the bottoms of plastic bottles, but we will reuse the other parts of the bottles for different instruments. We'll use these clip clop hooves during our Bible story. We'll pretend that the sound we make is the sound of animals praising God.

Soda Bottle Shofars (For All Ages)

- Give each child a bottle and a pair of safety scissors.

- Let the children cut strips from colored masking tape and then wrap the strips around the bottle. Be sure to have the children tape the cut edge at the bottom of the bottle. Leave the top of the bottle untaped.

- Demonstrate how to play the shofar. First, buzz your lips. Next put the shofar gently to your lips as you continue to buzz.

- **Say:** These are shofars. The shofar is a trumpet made from a ram's horn. It is used in Jewish and Christian worship. We will use these soda bottle shofars during our Bible story. We will pretend that the sound we make is the sound of people blowing trumpets to praise God.

Soda Cap Rattles (For Elementary Children)

- Give each child six to ten bottle caps, yarn, scissors, and six to ten beads.

- Have each child cut yarn into eight-inch lengths (one strand for every two bottle caps).

- Have each child thread a strand of yarn through a bottle cap (from the top side to the inside), and tie a bead to the end of the strand. This will keep the yarn from slipping back through the hole in the bottle cap.

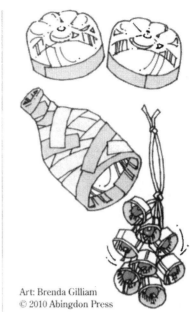

Art: Brenda Gilliam
© 2010 Abingdon Press

Prepare

✓ Cut off the bottom of a clean plastic bottle for each child.
✓ Use the bottom for the clip-clop hooves.
✓ Use the top for the shofars.
✓ Provide colored masking tape and safety scissors.
✓ Provide six to ten bottle caps and six to ten plastic beads for each child. Make sure the beads are large enough so that when added to the end of the yarn they will prevent the bead from pulling through the nail hole.
✓ Provide yarn and scissors.
✓ Use a hammer and a nail to punch holes in the top of each bottle cap. (Adults only!)
✓ *Note:* You can find more recycled instruments from *Make a Joyful Noisemaker* by Mark Burrows. ISBN: 0-687-49346-3

- Next, have each child thread the other end of the strand of yarn through another bottle cap and tie a bead to that end.

- Allow the children to continue until each of their strands has a bottle cap attached to both ends.

- Have the children tie the strands of yarn together in the middle, leaving the bottle caps loose enough to rattle together when shaken.

- Show the children how to hold their rattles by the yarn handle and bounce them in short up-and-down motions.

- **Say:** Did you notice that we have used every part of a soda bottle to make an instrument? We have the shofar from the top of the bottle, the clip-clop hooves from the bottom of the bottle, and the rattle from the cap. We have really recycled and reused plastic bottles.

Stars in orbit (for All Ages)

- **Ask:** Do you think the stars can praise God?

- **Say:** The person who wrote the psalm we will hear as our Bible story thought so. Stars praise God by being stars!

- Show the children the star ball made from aluminum foil.

- **Ask:** What do stars do? *(give light, travel in orbits)*

- **Say:** Stars move in orbits through the vast universe. Let's create orbit patterns for these stars.

- Have the children stand in a circle and raise one hand.

- Call out the name of a child with her or his hand up and gently toss him or her a star. Have the other children keep their hands raised. This will tell the group who has not had a turn catching the ball. The children may put their hands down once their names have been called.

- The child who caught the first star now calls out the name of another child in the circle and throws that child the star. Tell the children that they must remember who they throw the star to because it will become the permanent orbit.

- Continue throwing the star until everyone has caught the ball from someone. This completes the orbit.

- Start the orbit over again, throwing the star in the same pattern around the circle. Remind the children to call out the children's names before tossing the star.

Prepare
- ✓ Provide clean, used aluminum foil.
- ✓ Crumple the aluminum foil into a ball to represent a star.

Large Group

Bring all the children together to experience the Bible story. Blow a soda bottle shofar (see page 55) to alert the children to the large group time. Use the transition activity to move the children from the interest groups to the large group area.

Begin the Green Celebration (Transition Activity)

- Signal large group time.

- Have the children stop what they are doing in their interest groups and get ready to welcome guests to large group time and the celebration.

- Encourage the children to take their visitors to see the art gallery.

- Help the children sell their art work and the necklaces. Let parents and visitors know why the children are raising money.

- Offer the compost cups (see page 54) for refreshments. Remember to use reusable spoons.

- Talk about composting with parents and visitors (see pages 54–55).

Hear, See, and Act the Story of Creation

- Invite visitors to join the children for large group time.

- Lead the children and visitors in singing one or more of the "Recycle Songs."

- **Say:** Let's play a game. The object of the game is to see how many things from creation we can name in one minute. First, I will call out a letter of the alphabet. Then I will throw this recycled foil ball to someone. Whoever catches the ball quickly names something God created that starts with the letter I called out, and then throws the ball back to me. For example, if I call out "C," then you might say "cat" or "conch shell." Each time someone throws the ball back to me, I will call out a different letter and throw the ball to someone else.

- Play the game for several minutes.

- **Say:** Our Bible story is from Psalm 148. It is a song of praise for God, the Creator. In fact, the psalmist, the person who wrote the psalm, tells each part of creation to praise God.

- **Ask:** How do you think the sun or a tree praises God?

- **Say:** God created the sun to come up every morning. God created trees to grow and give off oxygen. They praise God by doing what God created them to do. Let's listen to Psalm 148.

- Read the Psalm to the group.

- **Say:** Let's hear the Psalm again and add sound effects with our bodies and our recycled instruments.

Prepare

✓ Provide CEV Bibles.

✓ Provide clean, used aluminum foil.

✓ Crumple the aluminum foil into a ball.

✓ Provide the instruments made earlier along with the candy wrapper instrument made in Week 5 (see pages 52–53).

✓ Provide the "Recycle Songs" (pages 4–5) song sheets.

- Hand out the musical instruments made in the interest groups. Explain that everyone will use either an instrument or a body part to represent the sound of something named in the psalm. Instruct the children to practice making the sounds as you name each item:

  Praise the Lord from the heavens! (shofar)
  Praise him, sun and moon! (rub hands together)
  Praise the Lord from sparkling waters! (bag instrument from Week 5)
  Praise the Lord, fire and rain (wind noises)
  Praise the Lord, rugged mountains! (stomp feet)
  Praise the Lord, fruit trees and cedars! (bottle cap rattles)
  Praise the Lord, tigers and bears! (clip clop hooves)
  Praise the Lord, seagulls and parrots! (cluck tongue)
  Praise the Lord, rulers and presidents! (clap hands)

- Read the "Psalm 148 Sound Effects Story" (page 61) and direct the children to make the sounds as indicated.

- Hand out the Bibles to the children.

- **Say:** Find Psalm 148. Now find the little number 13. Look at the words as I read the verse: "All creation, come praise the name of the LORD. Praise his name alone. The glory of God is greater than heaven and earth" (Psalm 148:13, CEV).

- **Ask:** Why does the psalmist think creation should praise God? *(God is greater than heaven and earth.)*

- **Say:** Our Bible verse tells us to take care of the earth. Let's race to find our verse. Who wants to come up front?

- Choose four to six children to come up front. They may bring their Bibles or you may give them Bibles when they are on stage.

- Pair the children in teams of two. If you have older and younger children, pair an older child with a younger child. Each pair needs a Bible.

- **Say:** When I say, "Go!" work together with your partner to find the verse. As soon as you find the verse, raise your hand. Are you ready? Find Psalm 8:6. Set. That's Psalm 8:6. Go!

- Encourage all the children to cheer as the partners work together to find the verse.

- Have the first pair to raise their hands, read the verse.

- Thank the children who came to the front and have them sit down.

- **Ask:** What is our big responsibility? *(to rule over everything God made)*

- Thank the guests for joining in the "Green Celebration."

- Dismiss the children and their guests to the small groups.

Small Groups

Divide the children into small groups. You may organize the groups around age-levels or around readers and nonreaders. Keep the groups small with a maximum of ten children in each group. You may need to have more than one of each group.

Young Children

- Have the children and their guests sit down around the table or in a circle.

- Open your Bible to Psalm 148.

- **Ask:** What were some of the parts of creation that were told to praise God in the psalm?

- As a group, come up with as many things as you can from the story that were called to praise God. (At least thirty different things are mentioned.)

- **Ask:** What is the one major reason why creation should praise God?

- **Say:** One way people praise God is by taking care of God's creation.

- Give each child, family group, or guest a pledge card (page 64) and a pencil.

- Read the pledge card to the group.

- Have each child, family group, or guest make a check beside each activity that they promise to do to take care of the earth.

- Encourage each participant to sign the pledge card.

- **Ask:** Do you remember the very first time we met, when you drew the pictures of a Caretaker of God's Creation?

- Look at the pictures from Week 1 (see pages 12–13).

- **Say:** You had different ideas and images of what a caretaker would look like. Well, I have a secret to tell you. That first week, I also had an image of what a Caretaker of God's Creation would look like. In fact, my image was an image that reminds me a lot of God and the love God shows to us. I want you to take my image with you, so I have these gifts for you. Open your gifts and you will see what I think a Caretaker of God's Creation looks like.

- Pass around the reusable bag. Have each child reach in the bag and take a hand mirror.

- **Say:** On the back of your mirror are the letters COGC. They stand for "Caretaker of God's Creation." Whenever you look in your mirror, remember how much God treasures who you are and what you have to offer the world.

- Read the "Caretaker of God's Creation Covenant" (see page 64). Have the children repeat each line after you.

- Close with prayer.

Prepare

- ✓ Provide: a Bible, pens or pencils, a permanent marker, and a reusable bag.

- ✓ Provide a small hand mirror for each child.

- ✓ Use a permanent marker to write the letters COGC on the back of each mirror.

- ✓ Place the mirrors in the reusable bag.

- ✓ Provide the pictures made during small group time in Week 1 (see pages 12–13).

- ✓ Photocopy the pledge card (page 64) for each family group.

- ✓ Reuse "God's Creation Covenant" (page 64).

Elementary Children

- Have the children and the guests sit down around the table or in a circle.

- Open your Bible to Psalm 148.

- **Ask:** What were some of the parts of creation that were told to praise God in the psalm?

- As a group, come up with as many things as you can from the story that were called to praise God. (At least thirty different things are mentioned.)

- **Ask:** What is the one major reason why creation should praise God?

- **Say:** One way people praise God is by taking care of God's creation.

- Give each child, family group, or guest a pledge card (page 64) and a pencil.

- Read the pledge card to the group.

- Have each child, family group or guest make a check beside each activity that they promise to do to take care of the earth.

- Encourage each participant to sign the pledge card.

- **Say:** Over the last several weeks, we have learned many ways to help care for God's creation.

- **Ask:** Do you remember the very first time we met, when you drew the pictures of a Caretaker of God's Creation?

- Look at the pictures from Week 1 (see pages 12-13).

- **Say:** You had different ideas and images of what a caretaker would look like. Well, I have a secret to tell you. That first week, I also had an image of what a Caretaker of God's Creation would look like. In fact, my image was an image that reminds me a lot of God and the love God shows to us. I want you to take my image with you, so I have these gifts for you. Pull out your gifts and you will see what I think a Caretaker of God's Creation looks like.

- Pass around the reusable bag. Have each child reach in the bag and take a hand mirror.

- **Say:** On the back of your mirror are the letters COGC. They stand for "Caretaker of God's Creation." Whenever you look in your mirror, remember how much God treasures who you are and what you have to offer the world.

- Hand out "Caretaker of God's Creation Covenant" (page 64).

- Read the covenant with the children. Send the covenant home with them.

- Close with prayer.

Prepare

- ✓ Provide: a Bible, pens or pencils, a permanent marker, and a reusable bag.

- ✓ Provide a small hand mirror for each child.

- ✓ Use a permanent marker to write the letters COGC on the back of each mirror.

- ✓ Place the mirrors in the reusable bag.

- ✓ Provide the pictures made during small group time in Week 1 (see pages 12–13).

- ✓ Photocopy the pledge card (page 64) for each family group.

- ✓ Reuse "God's Creation Covenant" (page 64).

Creation's Song of Praise

by Daphna Flegal

Praise the name of the Lord.
Praise the name of the Lord.
All creation jump on board,
Praise the name of the Lord!

Praise God in the heavens,
All angels way up high.
Praise God, sun and moon,
By shining in the sky.

Praise the name of the Lord.
Praise the name of the Lord.
All creation jump on board,
Praise the name of the Lord!

Praise God in the seas,
All creatures of the deep.
Praise God, stormy wind,
By blowing as we sleep.

Praise the name of the Lord.
Praise the name of the Lord.
All creation jump on board,
Praise the name of the Lord!

Praise God, rolling hills,
And mountains standing tall.
Praise God, trees and plants,
By growing, one and all.

Praise the name of the Lord.
Praise the name of the Lord.
All creation jump on board,
Praise the name of the Lord!

Praise God, creeping things,
And birds that fill the air.
Praise God, fox and wolf,
By howling from your lair.

Praise the name of the Lord.
Praise the name of the Lord.
All creation jump on board,
Praise the name of the Lord!

Praise God, every nation,
And every king and queen.
Praise God, young and old,
By keeping God's earth green.

Praise the name of the Lord.
Praise the name of the Lord.
All creation jump on board,
Praise the name of the Lord!

Psalm 148 Sound Effects Story

Play the shofars.
Praise the Lord from the heavens!
Praise the Lord from the skies!
All his angels, come praise the Lord!

Rub hands together.
Praise the Lord, sun and moon!
Praise the Lord, twinkling stars!
For God spoke and fixed their place in the sky.

Play the bag instrument (from Week 5).
Praise the Lord from sparkling waters!
Praise the Lord, fish and sea creatures!
Let every whale sing a song of praise!

Make wind noises.
Praise the Lord, fire and rain!
Praise the Lord, stormy wind!
Each falling snowflake, come praise the Lord!

Stomp feet.
Praise the Lord, rugged mountains!
Praise the Lord rolling hills!
Let red clay and sandy soil praise the Lord!

Shake bottle cap rattles.
Praise the Lord, fruit trees and cedars!
Praise the Lord, flowering plants!
Let sunflowers turn their faces to the Lord!

Play clip clop hooves.
Praise the Lord, tigers and bears!
Praise the Lord, running deer!
Elephants and oxen, come praise the Lord!

Cluck tongues.
Praise the Lord, seagulls and parrots!
Praise the Lord, scurrying mice!
Let hummingbirds hum their praise to the Lord!

Clap hands.
Praise the Lord, rulers and presidents!
Praise the Lord, people of the earth!
Let people of all ages praise the Lord!

Praise the Lord!

Danger Signs

This skull says, "Don't drink me, I'm poison!"

This sign says, "I'm full of germs and I can make you sick!"

This flame says, "I catch on fire easily!"

This sign says "I'm radioactive. I can make your hair fall out!"

This exploding bomb says, "Watch out! I like to blow things up!"

Triangle Pattern

organizations

Defenders of Wildlife

Conserves imperiled wildlife and wild lands. Your adoption donation will immediately be put to use where it is most needed to achieve these goals.
(800) 385-9712
www.WildlifeAdoption.org

The Children's Alliance for Protection of the Environment (CAPE)

A $100.00 donation will protect one acre of rainforest.

Richard W. Fox
CAPE Rainforest Program
Route 1, Box 246B
Rixeyville, VA 22737
(703) 937-5233

Arbor Day Foundation

Become a member, buy trees, or donate money to help with replanting forests.
(888) 448-7337
www.arborday.org

Nike's Reuse a Shoe

Collect worn out athletic shoes (any brand) for Nike's Reuse a Shoe program. The shoes are recycled into "Nike Grind." This material is used to make things like playground floors. There are strict guidelines, so check the website before taking any action.
www.nikereuseashoe.com

Caretaker of God's Creation Covenant

I am a caretaker of God's creation.
I help care for the world by giving.
I give my time to learn about God and the Bible.
I give my heart by loving those around me, even when it's hard.
I give myself by sharing my talents with others.
I give my gifts and money to share with those in need.
I give my hands by caring for others and protecting the earth.
I give my desire by wanting less and offering more.
I give all of me to help God care for the world.
I am a caretaker of God's creation.

Written by Suzann Wade © 2004 Abingdon Press.

I pledge to:

❏ recycle newspaper.

❏ turn off the water when
    I brush my teeth.

❏ take short showers.

❏ use both sides of paper.

❏ recycle glass, plastic,
    and aluminum.

❏ turn off lights when
    I leave the room.

❏ use cloth shopping bags.

❏ compost food waste.

❏ protect endangered animals.

❏ walk or ride my bicycle
    when possible.

❏ plant a tree.

signed:

CPSIA information can be obtained at www.ICGtesting.com
Printed in the USA
LVOW110058300413

331470LV00002B/22/P